The Student's Guide
to
Good Writing

THE STUDENT'S GUIDE TO

GOOD WRITING

Building Writing Skills for Success in College

RICK DALTON
MARIANNE DALTON

College Entrance Examination Board
New York

To our parents—Herb and Nance, Bill and Marty—whose support and love have made this venture and all else possible.

In all of its book publishing activities the College Board endeavors to present the works of authors who are well qualified to write with authority on the subject at hand, and to present accurate and timely information. However, the opinions, interpretations, and conclusions of the authors are their own and do not necessarily represent those of the College Board; nothing contained herein should be assumed to represent an official position of the College Board or any of its members.

Copies of this book are available from your local bookseller or may be ordered from College Board Publications, Box 886, New York, New York 10101-0886.

Editorial inquiries concerning this book should be directed to Editorial Office, The College Board, 45 Columbus Avenue, New York, New York 10023-6992.

Library of Congress Catalog Number: 89-085765
ISBN: 0-87447-353-5

Printed in the United States of America

9   8   7   6   5   4   3   2   1

Contents

Acknowledgments

Many more names than ours should appear on the cover of this book because it represents the collective energy of so many.

Hundreds of teachers and students took time to reflect on their writing and to share their writing experiences. For this we are grateful. We especially want to thank those who helped us with our own writing: Karen Boyden, Elaine Cissi, John Elder, Barbara Ganley, Dorthea Herrey, Randy Landgren, Meghan Laslocky, Ron Liebowitz, Sarah Martell, John McCardell, Terry Plum, Elizabeth Wilcox, Bill Wright, and Mary Ruth Yoe.

Dan Brigante and Cindy Pidgeon provided invaluable technological support, and the kindness and professionalism of our editor, Carolyn Trager, gave us the confidence we needed to survive the endeavor.

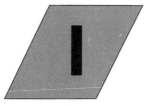

What
to
Expect

Listen to Annette, Sarah, and Matt as they reflect on becoming college writers. Their experiences are echoed by hundreds of other students.

ANNETTE: I call my first college paper "my freshman disaster." I was convinced that after Advanced Placement English and American history I could dash off an acceptable three-page paper in one evening. I sat poised at my word processor. Certainly this would insure the paper's looking good. How could any professor question the authority or competence of a neatly presented paper? The answer was "easily." In high school I had occasionally let my father proofread my essays, but usually I didn't want to risk having to make corrections. In college, I changed my ways.

MATT: The trauma of a C− was overwhelming. I had never received anything lower than a B, even in my honors courses. What went wrong with my first essay set me on the road to making things right with the rest of my college writing. Comma errors, mixed metaphors, misspellings, vague wording, scattered and underdeveloped ideas, lack of supporting evidence/details, typos, inadequate projections/conclusions, and absence of focus were some of the weaknesses noted in the margins of the paper. At that point, I realized how much I needed to learn about writing. This was my first step toward becoming a good writer.

SARAH: I always got frustrated when I wrote in high school because I couldn't make the writing perfect the first time. I was convinced that I couldn't write. I was too shy to ask for help from teachers, and I thought getting help from friends was cheating. At college, my junior counselor told me about peer tutors and the campus writing center. When I finally got it through my head that getting help didn't mean I was stupid, I was able to go to the writing

3

center. There I learned about the writing process; suddenly I didn't feel so helpless. At the center, I learned how to brainstorm and freewrite, how to write a rough draft, and how to revise my writing. It took time, but what a difference in my grades and how I felt about myself as a writer!

This book will not necessarily save you from these experiences, but it will help you know what to expect in college. With this knowledge, you can enter college with more confidence. For, as one student explained, "I always wondered if I would be able to do the work in college. To me, work meant writing. I knew I could read, but could I write?"

The Student's Guide to Good Writing can also help you learn to talk about your writing and to make your writing stronger. As Stephen, a college junior, puts it, "The process of improving your writing is more than making a few spelling corrections and copying over your paper a couple of times."

Our experience and research—including interviews and surveys of more than 300 students and teachers in high school and college—show that good writing goes beyond the technical aspects of structure and grammar. This is not to say that these components are unimportant. College professors agree that "students should arrive on campus understanding paragraph and essay structure, knowing grammar, and being able to develop a thesis." They suggest students bring handbooks, grammar guides, and stylebooks to college for technical advice.

As an aspiring college writer, you need another resource; one that outlines and presents the range of writing expectations in college. You need a book that offers specific advice about the writing process—prewriting, drafting, revising—and about word processing because, as one professor explains, "word processors have revolutionized writing." You need a book that defines writing terms and shows you how to develop an individual writing "voice" and "style." You need a book that explains how to use boldness to energize a grammatically correct essay that nevertheless is "dull."

The Student's Guide to Good Writing initiates a journey of self-exploration to ease your transition from high school to college writing. Through the words and writings of both college students and professors, this book demystifies the world of college writing by letting you know what to expect as a college writer.

The first four chapters focus on the writing you will do in college: the main ingredients, how you write, and what you will write.

Chapter 2 defines the standards of good college writing. You will explore the "Big Seven," seven elements that professors believe are essential for effective writing. These accompany a discussion of how writing expectations change as a student moves from high school to college. A professor who has taught in both high school and college describes high school writing as "a mile wide and an inch deep." College students agree that the major difference between the two writing worlds can be measured in intensity; college writing becomes narrower and deeper. Dawn, an Amherst College junior, explains her professors' demands for more analysis: "They keep asking me to look deeper. I think I've provided enough explanation and then they want more."

In Chapter 3 you will learn about the writing process. Most professors urge you to develop a personal writing plan so that your writing follows a series of steps. In this way, your papers evolve over time rather than in one frantic writing session. You will learn to think on paper and develop thoughts into a polished product. "It took me a long time to realize that each word and sentence didn't have to be perfect the first time I wrote them. This realization, more than any other, helped me become a college writer; I wish I had learned it in high school," writes a sophomore from the University of Connecticut.

Chapter 4 explores the writing formats most often required in college, including recommendations for writing journals, essay-test responses, reports, analytical essays, and composition assignments. Learning these different formats will save you countless hours of trying to figure out "what professors mean." Although no two professors have the same expectations, knowing the difference between these formats will help you ask questions about the particulars of an assignment. "I am always more receptive to students who don't appear totally helpless when faced with a writing assignment. I want students to ask me specific questions and not to throw up their hands in despair and ask 'what do you want'," insists a writing professor in Texas.

Chapter 5 helps you understand the different writing conventions for each academic subject area. You will explore the impact of a different audience on voice, form, content, and style in the humanities, the natural and social sciences, in foreign languages, and in business and technology. Samples of writing assignments will allow you to examine requirements in each of the disciplines. You will discover how writing for biology is both similar to and different from writing for English. Both biologists and English professors want clear, concise writing. However, biologists "don't want your lab report to be full of metaphors and clever phrases; they want facts about procedure and results," as a premed student from Colgate University has learned.

Chapter 6 presents ways to improve your writing during high school and summer vacations and while at college. Through individual initiative, college writing centers, and the computer, you can become a proficient writer. A high school senior from Virginia raises important questions: "I know that I need help with my writing. What can I do before I get to college? What can I do about getting help in college?"

Chapter 6 looks at ways you can prepare for college

writing during high school and summer vacations. There are myriad opportunities for you to improve your writing, to gain a sense of the demands of college-level writing before you actually enroll. Gigi, a student from a rural Georgia high school, wrote only one paper between her freshman and senior years in high school. Fearing what this could mean, she applied and was accepted to the Governor's Institute on the Arts. She is convinced that without those six weeks of intensive writing instruction, she would have struggled in college.

In recent years, colleges and universities have opened centers to help students with their writing. Chapter 7 introduces you to some of the services that can help you develop good writing practices, ranging from peer tutors to writing labs. These resources offer support to the writer in the same way that athletic trainers offer support to athletes. Sometimes there is a quick writing fix, like a writing "ice pack." Other times, it takes a slow, steady revision process along the lines of daily physical therapy. Either way, the relationship supports healthy writing.

Computers have revolutionized writing. In Chapter 8, students describe how they use computers to improve their writing. Focusing on the Big Seven, you will learn how word processing helps in these specific writing areas. As one student notes, "Everything I want is there on the screen in front of me before it even hits the paper. I get my thoughts down quicker, so I have more time to draft and revise." There are pitfalls in word processing and these will be discussed as well.

Chapter 9 goes beyond survival and addresses risk taking, style, voice, and confidence. It examines what is needed to take the next step, how to go beyond writing papers that are merely technically correct. It also looks at writing in the final college years and at how the skills you develop at that time can lead to lifelong good writing habits and practices.

In Chapters 10 and 11, college students and professors

will talk to you about writing expectations and require-ments, respectively. By focusing on the most frequently asked questions about college writing, you will discover that all college writing assignments are not 25 pages long and that professors *are* accessible and want to help you become a better writer. College professors also offer enter-ing freshmen inside information and advice on writing. Their recommendations will give you the inside track when it comes to college writing. By knowing what to expect, you can confront your writing head on. You will be able to spend more time writing and less time worrying.

2

Writing
for
College

Elaine, a college freshman, burst into her college adviser's office. "I was a good writer in high school," she complained, "and now my professor says I'm confusing and disjointed, and I have to revise this before he'll even grade it!" She threw her paper, thoroughly marked in red ink, on her adviser's desk and asked him to explain why the professor had written, "You grapple with the essential ideas." She sought some redeeming evaluation and some helpful hints from her adviser on how "to turn dynamic ideas into understandable ones."

When the adviser read the paper, he recognized that Elaine had some provocative ideas to communicate but still had to develop the skills for expressing them clearly. In her adviser's office, Elaine had her first lesson in the differences between high school and college writing. She learned from her adviser that her professor respected a confused, interesting paper more than a dry, organized one. That was why he often wrote "please revise" in bold red ink on the intriguing, disjointed essays, and gave C's to the orderly but less interesting ones. The professor had once commented to Elaine's adviser, "What's the use of organization if there's nothing there to organize?"

Elaine's feelings of frustration and helplessness are not unique. Many students whose high school essays earned high grades find themselves in Elaine's painful situation when they start getting back their first college assignments. There are several explanations for this. Rebecca Howard, director of Colgate University's Interdisciplinary Writing Program, believes that "what works well for a writer in high school, even what is taught in Advanced Placement English, is only preparation for college writing." To become a successful writer of college material, you need to be flexible and willing to learn more about writing. As one college student sums it up, "You've got to leave your ego at home if you want to become a good writer!"

Good college writing, according to faculty across the country, requires attention to seven elements:

1. Logic

2. Clarity

3. Diction

4. Audience

5. Boldness

6. Elaboration

7. Mechanics

Becoming familiar with these terms can help you analyze your own writing and take a first step toward improving it. Beyond this, knowing these terms will help you communicate with professors and peers. One professor observes that the greatest writing strength students can have is the "ability to discuss their writing using conventional terms of grammar and composition."

Many college students whom we surveyed identified rewriting as their most difficult academic challenge. They explained that it is often difficult to rewrite an essay be-

---

The Big Seven

1. Logic:	The ordering of ideas that leads to a cohesive statement.
2. Clarity:	The clearness with which you convey your thoughts and ideas.
3. Diction:	The words you choose when you write.
4. Audience:	The people for whom you are writing.
5. Boldness:	The vitality and daring that drives your writing.
6. Elaboration:	The careful way in which you develop and expand your ideas.
7. Mechanics:	The structural parts of your writing.

cause they don't understand the terms professors use. Becoming familiar with these terms, therefore, will help you avoid this communication gap.

Logic

The cornerstone of good college writing is *logic*. Logic builds a sequence of ideas that, in turn, conveys a decisive and reasonable argument. Further, logic establishes and maintains a focus.

Beginning with each sentence and then each paragraph, good writing must be logical. Sentences must be easy to follow and must flow from one idea to another, contributing to a central idea. The overall point must be stated clearly and directly at the outset. For an English assignment on poetic imagery, a sophomore began his paper: "Robert Frost's imagery in 'After Apple Picking' creates a mood of preslumber calm." This statement defines the scope of the paper: the writer will focus on images in a Frost poem that create a mood of "preslumber calm." The sentence, or thesis statement, serves as the road sign that tells us exactly where we are going.

The thesis statement frames and guides the logic. To the football player, the thesis is the quarterback's play. To the business person, the thesis is the sales strategy. To the diplomat, the thesis is the peace objective. Every move, every promotional, every agreement is keyed logically to that original statement.

Following what one philosophy professor terms "cogent lines of reasoning," you should select evidence that is relevant to your thesis. A good writer weaves together pertinent, concrete details—patiently, not hurriedly—to form an integrated statement. Merely stringing together sentences that embody similar ideas does not necessarily lead to logic. While sitting with her adviser, Elaine learned that she had presented dynamic ideas. However, her ideas lacked the organization and the collection of evidence that make a careful point. She had not organized her ideas into sentences and paragraphs that, in the words of one writing professor, make a "strong case as strongly as possible."

Elaine's paper, written for a sociology class that focused on contemporary issues, began: "The American school system deserves a failing grade. Throughout the nation, children are rewarded for not learning. The national debt is a reflection of these same failings." After speaking with her adviser, Elaine realized that she had failed to substantiate several provocative statements and that the effect was a leap in logic. When she revised her paper, she gave examples of how students were rewarded for not learning, and she explained *how* the national debt was related to failings in the American educational system.

Several college faculty members and students we interviewed mentioned common misperceptions about what constitutes a well-written writing assignment. A paper that is "competent stylistically, but falls prey to an error in logic, is poorly written," explains the head of freshman writing at a large midwestern university.

In an essay written for a political science class, Bill, a first semester freshman, concluded: "The degrading treatment of Afghanistan's women and children by the Soviets illustrates the need to keep the Soviets out of Central America." This paper about Soviet influence in the Third World did not mention Central America until the concluding sentence. Inserting this point in the conclusion distracts the reader. Regardless of whether or not the Soviets should be kept "out of Central America," the impact of the final point is lost because of this lapse in logic.

A simple exercise can help you test for logic. Starting with your thesis statement, circle the key words (nouns and verbs) that organize your essay. Then, circle the key words in each of your topic sentences. There should be a correspondence between these circled words. For example, if your thesis statement reads, "Working conditions led the industrial workers to lobby for socialism," you would circle "working conditions," "lobby," and "socialism." When you test your topic sentences, you should find specific working conditions, possibly low wages, long hours, and poor health benefits; references to the "lobby," political strategies, even strikes; and the details of the resulting plan for "socialism." These topic sentences might introduce the specific contract components and the new labor–management relationship.

Once you have established that your paragraphs form a tight sequence of related ideas that lead to a natural conclusion, you can follow this same procedure within paragraphs. Underline the nouns and verbs in each of your sentences to be sure that each sentence is linked to its predecessor. These links will build a chain of logic both within and between paragraphs. This simple test could have saved Bill from weakening his paper with an illogical conclusion.

Clarity

In addition to using logic as the framework of your writing, you must convey your ideas simply and economically. George Orwell, in his essay, "Why I Write," says that "good prose is like a window pane." Indeed, good writing means that you make your ideas clear to the reader.

This is more than a rule of good composition. For, in the words of Brett Millier, professor of American literature at Middlebury College, good writing has the responsibility "to mean something and say what it means." To cloud your ideas by writing what college professors commonly call "pompous prose" is to shirk this responsibility. Beware of elaborate prose that sounds impressive but is incomprehensible. Good writing communicates with the reader and does not try to impress with obscure words and unnecessarily complex sentence structure.

"Always try for the simpler alternative," recommends Connecticut College professor Robert Askins. The following sentence, from a freshman history paper, lacks clarity: "The United States is not the only guilty party in the use of and experimentation with astounding amounts of nuclear power without being completely knowledgeable and taking all possible safety measures." The meaning of this sentence becomes clear when we reduce it to, "The United States is not alone in the negligent use of and experimentation with nuclear power." The meaning is obscured in the original, overwritten sentence. As a writer, your responsibility is to be clear.

Many students, when criticized for unclear or wordy writing, justify it as their "style." It is essential, however, for you to distinguish between personal style and affectation; never use style as an excuse to mask confusion. Karen, a college sophomore, relates how she felt intimidated by her intellectual surroundings, so she tried to put on "academic airs" in her writing. Karen used long, drawn out sentences filled with words selected from a thesaurus. She looks back at one paper and laughs when she reads: "The antihumanistic milieu totallistically permeated the nefarious epoch's sinister reaction." Fortunately, Karen's professor noticed her confusion and took her aside and urged her toward clarity.

In college, clear writing means clear thinking. In the early draft stage, when you first start to write a paper (steps are discussed in Chapter 3), your idea may be unclear. Through several drafts and over time, your writing gains clarity. College writing demands thoughtful prose, which comes from taking time to explore and make sense of an idea. Lack of time is not an excuse for unclear writing. Reza, now a college sophomore, talks about letting every paper she writes for her international politics courses sit for at least one or two days between drafts. "This is the only way I can check to see if my ideas are clear and make sense," she explains. "It is incredible how often I reread a draft and find whole sections that make absolutely no sense."

Diction

Clarity and diction are closely related. Clarity depends on diction—the words you choose. Indeed, precise words lead to forceful communication. As a college writer, therefore, you must demonstrate your knowledge and understanding of your subject through concise diction. You cannot hide behind big words that either don't fit or make the writing sound good but mean little. Clear, concise words linked tightly together will help you convince the reader that what you are saying is worth reading.

"A first step," urges an English professor at an Ivy League university, "is to leave your passive verbs and most of your adverbs at home." Instead of writing, as one college sophomore did, "The young peasant children were herded by the invaders," write: "The invaders herded the peasant children." The active voice forces direct communication by creating a visual image of the event. Almost without exception, the active voice engages the reader through sight, sound, taste, touch, and smell. Another example of the passive voice reads: "Radium was first discovered by Marie Curie." The meaning is not altered, but there is a change in impact with, "Marie Curie discovered radium." Not only does the active voice engage us, but the word "first" serves no purpose in the original example, only cluttering its effect.

A second step is to select the best word for the given situation. In our first example, the word *herded* creates a much stronger visual image than would, say, *gathered*. *Herded* also suggests the *way* the invaders treated the children. Because one *herds* cows but *gathers* eggs, *herd* is the better choice because it conveys the writer's critical point of view. In an essay on Babe Ruth, a college student wrote: "It was benign luck that allowed the Babe to become a hitter rather than a pitcher." The student used *benign* when he actually meant *good*, clouding the meaning of the sentence by his poor word choice.

A creative writing professor from a California university recommends underlining key nouns and verbs after writing your first draft, and then listing several synonyms to find the best word for that particular context. Many students report keeping their own dictionary of synonyms in a small notebook to increase their diction options. As you find new words, you may want to list them alphabetically under headings. For example, under the word *evil*, you might list *nefarious, malignant,* and *sinister*. Then, depending on the subject and the audience, you would select the appropriate word. You not only improve the diction of that particular essay, but you also create a list of word choices for the future.

"Beware the thesaurus," warns Jane, a sophomore from the University of New Hampshire. A dictionary is the better resource for diction because it describes appropriate usage. If you use a thesaurus, keep a dictionary nearby or cross-reference the synonyms to avoid embarrassing word choices. "I once tried to impress my literature professor," explains Jane, "by using the fancy word *dissipate* instead of the simple word *scatter*. A quick trip to the dictionary would have shown me that people *scatter*; they do not *dissipate* when they flee a storm."

Diction is important for another reason. A varied vocabulary will help you develop a confident writing voice. Your writing voice affects the way you come across to your reader; it can also be called a writer's tone. Voice or tone can be formal or informal, angry or controlled, biased or neutral. The words you choose and the way you arrange them create your voice. When you speak, you do the same thing; you choose your words to convey your anger, pleasure, or bias. When your word choice is specific, you communicate effectively with your reader. Unimpaired by vague or incorrect diction, your reader will respond positively to your writing. After all, it stands to reason that if your words are clear and accurate, your thinking must be clear and accurate, as well. Hence, good diction leads to a confident writing voice that leads, in turn, to positive reader reaction. This instills overall confidence in your writing ability.

One way to refine and explain your choice of words is through reading. Preparing to be a good writer involves being a good reader. Many college professors recommend a "reading regimen" to aspiring good writers. You might want to begin now by reading a newspaper every day, a magazine every week, and perhaps a book a month. A professor who often speaks to honors American history classes recommends that students read either *Time* or *Sports Illustrated*: "They capture student interest, and they provide wonderful models of good writing." Reading can improve your diction; it is the cornerstone of developing a sophisticated vocabulary free of jargon and colloquialisms.

Audience

The fourth element of good writing focuses on sensitivity to your reader. To become a good writer, you must know for whom you are writing. In college, it is often difficult to think of any audience other than the professor.

When a group of college sophomores was asked to define their most common audience they chimed in unison: "Professors! Professors! Professors!"

Knowledge of your audience is essential to the selection of details and language. Ask yourself the simple questions: Who? What? Where? Why? This will help you identify who your readers are, what you want to tell them, and why they might be interested in your ideas. After sizing up your audience, take time to anticipate the questions they might ask. By knowing the reader, you can figure out how to convey your point. Without this knowledge, the writer cannot select the appropriate voice or language.

It is your responsibility to establish a bond with the reader. Like any good relationship, the one between writer and reader takes time and commitment. Multiple drafts, with their inherent editing, allow the writer to zero in on the reader. In simple terms, you are trying to find a fit. You need to tailor your words to the person or persons for whom you are writing—no easy task. You begin by clarifying who your audience is.

Different audiences mean that you must make adaptations in your writing. (Chapter 5 explores this issue in greater detail.) You must look at each paper and try to evaluate it from your reader's perspective. For example, a summary writing assignment in biology is easier if you stop to realize that this piece is for your science professor. The science professor is a reader who expects a tightly sequenced response in specific scientific language. Now, if you're writing for a group of 10-year-olds, obviously the writing changes. Let's assume that you need to communicate the same set of scientific information that was written for the science professor to a fifth-grade class. The fifth graders will need verbal illustrations as well as definitions of such concepts as evolution, adaptation, and genetic strength. The science professor will need more specifics within these categories. As a good college writer, you will want to take time to work with your audience and not just write a generic response intended for everyone.

College writing assignments require versatility; varied audiences constantly force you to assess and reassess what you say and how you say it. Taking time to appraise your audience raises your consciousness, an important step toward becoming a successful lifelong writer.

Boldness

Good writing is characterized by a willingness to take risks, to be bold. Boldness reflects a conscious decision to surprise your audience. Ask yourself: "Would I rather read a dry, safe essay or one that teases and challenges me?"

High school is the place to discover and test your creative talents. College is the place to assert them. Steve Trombulak, a biology professor at Middlebury College, explains, "Good writing requires a large amount of personal energy. If the writing brings water to your eyes and makes your hands shake, it is good writing."

One professor urges his students to be bold from the outset of an assignment by selecting a creative topic. Dennis, a college sophomore, does this with his topic "Beyond War: An Abbreviated Pacifist Manifesto." Likewise, Carmen, a college junior, uses a bold first sentence when she declares, "American music has always faced an identity crisis." Both Dennis and Carmen effectively grab the attention of their readers.

Boldness requires a willingness to encounter new ideas and to challenge preconceptions. As stated earlier, college is the time to be comfortable with new audiences. A chemistry professor encourages her students to be bold, giving them the following assignment: "Look at the Chernobyl explosion not only as an American but also as a

Russian and as a world citizen." Modify your personal beliefs and place them in a new context. Realize that both Soviet and American scientists know about the explosive power of nuclear energy and try to figure out why both countries have still engaged in dangerous experimentation. Recognize both the positive and negative ways nuclear energy can be used and accept that nuclear energy may be here to stay (at least, during our lifetime). Now, take a deep breath and write a bold, fresh statement that resolves the duality. College writing takes on both sides and seeks to explore a complex idea through bold, creative argumentation.

Elaboration

Elaboration is the ability to develop and explore an idea. In the words of John McWilliams, an American literature professor, elaboration is "the ability to shape an argument that lasts beyond one paragraph." Troy, a writing tutor, offers this insight: "In high school, I thought elaboration was just more pages—padding. I've learned that it is not just *more*, but fresh examples that enhance and further explain your point."

A professor from the University of Virginia calls elaboration an "exhaustive search." When elaborating an idea or explanation, you explore many and varied possibilities; it is as if you are looking at an idea under a microscope. In other words, you explore the nuances and subtleties of a subject. For example, in her paper on the identity crisis in American music, Carmen discusses several distinct styles—jazz, big band, and folk—and makes a case for quality, originality, and substance. Thoughtful and intelligent prose emanates from a sustained line of thought.

Carmen's explanation is detailed and developed rather than general and unsubstantiated.

Margaret Shirley, a writing instructor at the University of New Hampshire, tells her students that "when you reach a point in your writing where you say to yourself 'my reader will know what I mean' and you stop writing, you should instead write more." Your writer should understand "beyond a shadow of a doubt" the idea or subject about which you are writing. This keeps your writing from being general and undeveloped. In an environmental studies paper on the ozone layer, you want to do more than suggest that an international organization should solve the problem. You must clearly outline why and how this organization should function. You need to offer not only the philosophical reasons but the practical ones as well. What is your plan for financing the project? What is your plan for governance? How will you publicize the project? How will different countries take responsibility for and share in the burden of the crisis? Instead of answering each of these questions in a sentence or two, you should develop several paragraphs packed with data and evidence.

Elaboration requires more than supporting quotations. When you use quotations in your writing, you need to interpret them. The connections you make between quotations and your text demonstrate your thinking process and, in so doing, your understanding. A University of Michigan professor suggests that "the analysis should be at least twice as long as the quotation or data."

When should you stop writing? When does elaboration become padding? First, keep close to your thesis statement. Material or ideas that are not directly related to your thesis are superfluous. For example, if your thesis states that Depression photographs reflect endurance and dignity, your elaboration should explore only those ideas that enable you to draw a parallel between endurance and dignity. You should not "pad" your paper with biographies of the different photographers who took the pictures.

23

Often, professors will assign a specific length for a paper, thereby setting limits on your elaboration. You will have to control your discussion to fit the length. In a three-page paper, restrict your examination to one idea and explore it in depth rather than taking four or five ideas and discussing them in general terms to fill up the paper.

Elaboration is like making lasagna. Each layer of explanation and interpretation adds to the richness of the discussion in the same way that each layer of cheese, sauce, and noodles adds to the richness of the dish. First, make a statement. Then add several sentences that explore the idea. Then, go back and add several new sentences between each original sentence. In this way, you develop an idea to its fullest. You can even do this with paragraphs. Keep adding paragraphs that explore a dimension of the topic. If you develop ideas and explore all facets of your topic, whether a literary character or a political theory, your writing will reflect both depth and commitment.

As you become more skilled in developing a focus and a thesis statement for your writing, you will discover yet another avenue to elaboration. Writing a complex rather than a simple thesis will force you to elaborate. In a simple thesis addressing mob psychology, you might examine only the perspective of the victim or of the attacking mob. According to Kathleen Skubikowski, director of Middlebury's writing program, "The good writer explores the aggressor's story, as well." This forces you, the writer, to elaborate on the topic of mob psychology beyond a single point of view. Your thesis will then acknowledge both the victim and the attacker: "Driven by anger and the taunts of the crowd, the attacker became the victim." In your essay, it will be impossible for you not to elaborate on the complexity of this real-life situation.

The more skilled you become at elaboration, the more your writing will take you beyond the specific subject matter to explore your own ideas and values.

Mechanics

The seventh, and final, element of good writing is freedom from errors in spelling, grammar, punctuation, and other structural components. Professors want a written product that is polished and error-free. One professor comments, "Good writing is like a gourmet meal. But, even a gourmet meal suffers if it's cooked carelessly, in the same way that good ideas are sabotaged by mechanical errors."

The rules of grammar, like the ingredients in a gourmet meal, are important. Grammar and spelling don't have to be perfect in the first draft, but they should be by the time the final draft is submitted. As one student explains, "There is no way that you aren't mortified when a professor returns a paper with all sorts of spelling corrections. Even if these errors do not affect your paper's grade, they affect your reputation and self-respect." Some part of the writing process must include a grammar and spelling check.

With respect to mechanics, there is no universal competency level expected of all college freshmen. The level varies among and even within colleges and universities. There is, however, the common expectation that freshmen know the basics of language structure in written form, and one professor speaks for many others when he asserts, "I will not teach them to you in college." It is best to prepare for what will be expected in college by improving your skills now. College professors are eager to get beyond mechanical issues. Professor Williams of the University of Chicago's English department articulates the position of faculty nationwide: "So long as I don't have to spend time on matters of basic competence, I figure I can move young writers along in matters of structure and argumentation very quickly."

Professors may disagree about how to eliminate mechanical errors and become a competent writer. There is no disagreement, however, on the following: you need a style manual and/or a reference guide to grammar to which you can refer in your final editing. Two excellent texts are Strunk and White, *The Elements of Style* and Corbett, *The Little English Handbook*. A good writer does not cast his writing fate to the wind by making haphazard guesses about prepositions and pronouns or about acceptable sentence constructions.

Although few professors expect their students to spell perfectly, they do expect written assignments to be relatively error-free. There are plenty of resources to help you meet this expectation. A dictionary is essential and a grammar text is useful, since most include lists of commonly misspelled words, alerting you to possible pitfalls. Make use of the spell-check function if you're word processing. More than one college student recommends setting up a support network with a classmate or two. "Bill and I never would have made it through first semester if we hadn't been able to rely on each other for proofing and editing," writes one California sophomore. Mutual support systems are an essential part of good writing for many students. A circle of readers can help you strengthen logic, clarity, diction, boldness, elaboration, and voice. These readers can also point out questionable grammar, usage, or spelling. (At the end of Chapter 3, there is a form that might help you and your friends become better critical readers by focusing on the seven elements of good writing.) In addition, critiquing your peers' papers can help you hone your own writing skills.

There is no need to become paranoid about grammar and spelling. Clearly, mechanics are a good writer's responsibility, but keep in mind one professor's final bit of advice: "Try to be a creative reporter rather than a mechanical, duty-driven student." Maintain your perspective; don't sacrifice boldness for correctness.

You might be asking how a writer incorporates all of these good writing elements into one paper at one time. The key word here is *time*. Good writing does not happen in one sitting. You must come to college knowing how to plan and control your writing time. Chapter 3 will help you with this aspect of the writing process.

Writing
As a
Process

"Writing is the basic process of capturing on paper what goes on in my mind and in my heart. I write to get out what is inside," explains Leslie, a high school senior from California. Part of becoming a college writer is understanding how and why you write. Leslie describes writing as a "process" whereby she presents her ideas and feelings. This chapter exposes you to a process that will help *you* to present your ideas and feelings, as well as your knowledge. A writing process or a personal writing plan is an essential component of good writing. Just as a builder needs a blueprint to construct a solid building, you need a writing process to become a good writer.

Not so long ago, teachers were primarily concerned with the final written product. Few writers talked about how they wrote; few teachers introduced students to the steps that writers take to produce a polished piece of prose; and few students understood that rewriting compositions was a natural step and not a punishment. Cristina, a college freshman from the Southwest, hesitated to talk to people about her writing: "I was too self-conscious to ask for help, and I was terrified that I would have to rewrite my paper."

Because she had not developed a personal writing plan early on in college, Cristina felt alone and intimidated by writing. Taking the time to develop a step-by-step writing process will help you move from an idea to a polished written product and also help you avoid Cristina's plight.

Many of your professors will refer to "prewriting," "drafting," and "revising," the steps in the writing process, and we will refer to and use this terminology here. Taking the time to become comfortable with these terms will help you become a college writer and save you time and anxiety.

Prewriting

"I would sit and stare at a blank piece of paper for hours. I felt I had to shape my ideas into sentences and paragraphs, right from the start. Prewriting techniques have helped me break my writer's block," writes a student from the University of Maine.

Prewriting can include drawing, listing, mapping, talking, or simply thinking while chewing on the end of a pencil. Prewriting helps you explore your thoughts and can help you generate paper topics and thesis statements for analytical essays. In creative writing, prewriting could lead to the creation of a character or help you weave a tangled plot. Two common prewriting techniques are brainstorming and freewriting.

Brainstorming

Brainstorming helps you list and gather questions, words, phrases, pictures, and images associated with the topic. In this way, you can quickly fill a blank piece of paper with your ideas. Because there is no right or wrong, brainstorming is nonthreatening. It is the writing step that gives you the opportunity to consider many related subjects, ideas, and feelings. If you try to structure your ideas into perfect prose right from the start, you might lose other thoughts along the way. For example, in an environmental science course, you might be asked to address a solid waste issue. After an initial brainstorm, you find that your real interest is the commercial side of the issue. In a second, focused brainstorm, you follow the same process of listing, but this time, you keep yourself focused on commercial solid waste issues. At the end of this brainstorm, you should find yourself with several possible avenues of research and often an informal outline to help you organize a rough draft.

Freewriting

Freewriting, like brainstorming, knows no boundaries—structure and form are nonexistent. What counts is writing as much as you can about any ideas or thoughts you might have about a given subject: a science experiment you conducted, a poem or short story you read, a personal problem, world hunger or space travel. Through freewriting you will discover the different sides of an idea. This, in turn, can lead you to discover topics for essays, poems, and compositions.

You will often want to use your brainstorms for freewriting. For example, in the solid waste assignment, you might want to freewrite on the disposal of commercial solid waste. Through freewriting, you might discover that your primary interest is how industry and business are part of the problem and must be part of the solution. You might also see the consumer as the primary catalyst for making things happen. Had you begun researching and writing a draft without prewriting, you might not have discovered this bias until your paper was well under way and it was too late to turn back.

Prewriting is not limited to paper and pencil; you can just as easily brainstorm and freewrite on a computer. Many students say word processing offers important side benefits to prewriting. In college, Roy found himself with assignments due simultaneously. "I often felt overwhelmed by ideas. Finally, I realized that word processing and prewriting offered solutions. Now, if I'm in the middle of one paper and get an idea for another, I add this brainstorm to a sheet in my notebook or, better yet, create a new file on my computer disk. This not only helps me organize my time, but it also keeps several writing assignments alive at once."

Drafting

Think of your first draft as a soccer or field hockey scrimmage. A first draft is like an athletic scrimmage because both have all the elements of the real thing, but they offer an opportunity to make mistakes and corrections before anything counts. Therefore, as soon as you are confident about your writing focus, create a structure for your ideas.

A first draft might have only a rough thesis statement and topic sentences followed by facts and data that support your argument. For example, in the solid waste assignment, your first draft might be:

- **Rough Thesis:** *Without the support of business and industry, solid waste will continue to be a major environmental threat.*

- **Topic Sentence 1:** *Overpackaging produces unnecessary solid waste.* In this paragraph, you would present statistics revealing amounts of Styrofoam, glass, plastic, and other nonbiodegradables used by industry. You would also describe what these materials ultimately do to the environment.

- **Topic Sentence 2:** *When stores and other businesses use nonbiodegradable bags and wrapping, they add another layer to the solid waste heap.* In this paragraph, you would record problems associated with these forms of waste and recommend possible alternatives.

- **Topic Sentence 3:** *Industrial by-products are another environmental hurdle.* In this paragraph, you would chart industrial disposal of various by-products and explore the environmental impact of the disposal (for example, the disposal of the by-product whey by cheese factories).

- **Topic Sentence 4:** *Landfills cannot keep up with household trash, let alone commercial solid waste.* In this paragraph, you might outline the landfill crisis by documenting landfill closings, the expense of lining landfills and controlling leachates, and the amount of land available for landfills.

- **Topic Sentence 5:** *Consumers have the power to pressure commercial business and industry to address this serious environmental crisis.* In this paragraph, you might discuss consumers' economic strategies to combat the problem, citing instances in which consumers have made a difference. You might then conclude with a plan for a nationwide boycott of stores and businesses that do not take appropriate steps to curb solid waste.

In this first draft, logic is your first consideration. Your topic sentences and information are organized into a logical sequence. Grouping similar ideas and concepts will help you build paragraphs. After you have a working draft of rough paragraphs, you can begin building a logical sequence of sentences within these blocks.

Keep reminding yourself that good writing goes through multiple drafts. You should write a new draft after each revision step. In another draft, you might find that each of the paragraphs on the solid waste problem needs to be developed into two or three paragraphs to present an in-depth solid waste disposal plan that is substantiated and elaborated.

Revising

When you first begin revising, do not worry about correcting spelling and grammar. Instead, use the Big Seven to ask yourself questions about focus, logic, audience, clarity, boldness, and elaboration. Mechanics, assuredly, is part of the revision process. Many writers, however, feel that this is the primary function of revision, when instead it is the final step.

Questions can spark a comprehensive revision by helping you check for both writing strengths and weaknesses. In Chapters 4 and 5, you will see how different assignments and different academic disciplines emphasize different writing skills. Before you begin a writing assignment and frame revision questions, establish the criteria of both the assignment and the professor. In many instances, you will be able to use the Big Seven, but you must be sensitive to the nuances of assignments and individual biases of professors. Keep in mind that a creative writing assignment will require a different checklist than an analytical essay or a report.

One way to begin evaluating your writing is to read it aloud either to yourself or to someone else. You are likely to find that your ear recognizes good writing. As you read, listen for some of the seven elements listed in Chapter 2. You may, for instance, want to listen for lapses in logic— places where the writing seems to lose its focus or sentences that are unrelated to the thesis. In the paper on commercial solid waste, for example, the focus is industrial responsibility. Therefore, you would listen to be sure that the topic sentences relate to that focus.

Try to include other people in your revision process. Ask a friend to check your writing for audience and diction. Or, have a friend go over a draft to look for passive verbs and commas. Even better, ask a peer to critique your paper using the Big Seven Checklist found at the end of this chapter. Involving others can help eliminate the feelings of isolation experienced by many student writers.

As you revise your writing, target a specific element. If you are working with a writing tutor or having a conference with a professor, identify your reason for revising. Never revise for all of the Big Seven at once. For example, if you are checking for such elements as audience, boldness, and elaboration, you are likely to, in the words of one college student, "become revision blind" and ineffectively screen all three. Take each one separately or combine two. After each session, write or print out a new draft. In Chapter 8, you will read how word processing can make this step in the writing process more efficient, or as one student claims, "200 percent faster."

A Big Seven revision checklist is included at the end of this chapter. Following the steps outlined below, use the checklist with a friend, a peer tutor, or a professor to focus your revision.

Revising for the Big Seven

1. **Logic:** As soon as you have a first draft in hand, read it aloud and focus on logic. You will be amazed how much easier it is to hear lapses in logic than to see them. When you have paragraphs that present a sequence of ideas leading to a logical conclusion, you can begin fine-tuning them.

   Check to see that sentences are linked together so that they form a cohesive statement as outlined in the Logic section. Test paragraphs for specifics. Without a body of facts, examples, quotations, and/or data, your argument will be too general. You need this material to build a logical case. Judy, now a Princeton junior, talks about the strategy for ensuring logic that she learned in high school. "My English teacher kept suggesting that we were lawyers trying to prove innocence or guilt. We were to think of our paragraphs as witnesses and the specifics of the paragraphs as their testimony. A witness could speak for one paragraph or several, depending on the role of that witness. To this day, I use this model to sort out the logic of my papers."

2. **Clarity:** Now, read the paper aloud or have a friend read it aloud to you and listen for unclear sections, sentences, or words. Mark or circle vague areas so that you can go back and sort them out. If you have used technical terminology, be sure that you have defined your terms.

3. **Diction:** If you hear vague or imprecise terms, use the test outlined in the Diction section below to gain control of the language. Depending on the clarity of the writing, you might be able to combine steps two and three into one revision.

4. **Audience:** Ask your listener to describe your audience. Are there places where you shift your writing voice? If there are, ask yourself: Why am I writing this piece and for whom? If your listener feels comfortable with the audience or can identify with them, you probably are in good shape.

5. **Boldness:** At this point, you will have produced at least two drafts of the essay, report, composition, or story. Now, see if your reader is awake. Has the writing put him to sleep or is he intrigued with what you have said? Are *you* still excited about what you have written or are you bored with the content or style? If you decide that what you have written is dull, add some spice to it. Are your verbs strong? Are your topic sentences hard-hitting?

6. **Elaboration:** Have you sustained your argument? Is there enough about each of your points to convince your reader that you know what you are talking about? Can you sink your teeth into meaty arguments? Elaboration can be addressed at different points: when you are looking at logic and toward the end, when you have sorted out diction and clarity. Don't confuse elaboration with length. If you do, you might tend to repeat yourself rather than develop your major ideas.

7. **Mechanics:** Unless you are using a word processor with spelling and grammar checks, don't try to polish a final draft for spelling, grammar, and punctuation by yourself. It is hard to catch little mistakes. Here, you need a friend to scrutinize your writing, not for content but for mechanics.

As we have mentioned in this chapter, you will not find one set of questions that applies to every piece of writing. Often, you will need to develop a different checklist for a short story than for a chemistry lab report. With the short story, you might have to adapt the list to include creative terms. The following checklist will help you with analytical essays. Professors and writing tutors can help you set up revision criteria. If, however, you are left on your own, this list will keep you from feeling abandoned during the revision process.

The Big Seven Checklist

	Y	N
1. Logic		
Is there a focal or thesis statement?	☐	☐
Do the paragraphs follow a logical sequence?	☐	☐
Do the sentences follow a logical sequence?	☐	☐

	Y	N
Are there facts, specifics, details, reasons that prove the thesis?	☐	☐

2. Clarity

	Y	N
Are there places in the essay that don't make sense?	☐	☐
Are there sentences that are unclear?	☐	☐
Are the ideas stated simply?	☐	☐
Is the terminology clearly defined?	☐	☐

3. Diction

	Y	N
Are verbs active or passive?	☐	☐
Are there places where one word could replace several?	☐	☐
Are words misused?	☐	☐
Do the words just sound good or do they mean something?	☐	☐
Have words been repeated or have appropriate synonyms been used?	☐	☐

4. Audience

	Y	N
Who is the audience?	☐	☐
Is the writing voice consistent or does it shift?	☐	☐
Does the diction fit the audience?	☐	☐

5. Boldness

	Y	N
Does the topic have energy?	☐	☐
Does the essay have energy?	☐	☐
Does the diction have energy?	☐	☐

	Y	N

6. Elaboration

Has the topic been explored from all angles? ☐ ☐

Is the discussion detailed and developed? ☐ ☐

7. Mechanics

Are there errors in spelling? ☐ ☐

Are there errors in grammar? ☐ ☐

Are the sentences punctuated accurately? ☐ ☐

Conclusion

You will probably have to spend more time with Chapter 3, because developing a writing process and designing a personal writing strategy take thought, practice, and time. Do, however, take the following thought with you and keep repeating it each time you write. Accepting this truth will free you from feelings of despair about your writing and will allow you to accept the writing challenge.

"Writing is nothing more than rewriting." And, remember:

- Good writers draft and revise.

- Good writers share their writing.

- Good writers talk about writing and how they write.

- Good writers know that rewriting shows strength, not weakness.

- Good writers have several people read their drafts to ask questions and make revision suggestions.

Writing
in
College

Chapter 4 focuses on the five different types of writing you are likely to encounter in college: journals, compositions, reports, analytical essays, and essay tests. This chapter defines these forms, discusses how to approach each form, and explores common problems students experience with each.

A Brooklyn College professor bluntly describes his role in developing college writers: "My aim is to show my students the rules of the game and to get them to conform to those rules quickly." The "game" is learning how to write. In college you will learn how to play the "game" by practicing the five different forms of writing.

Journals

The main difference between journals and the four other forms of writing discussed in this chapter is audience; you (and not your professor) are the primary audience in journal writing. Because of this, your diction can be informal. You can respond impulsively, and this freedom provides a way to improve your writing. Because journal writing is free-form, it offers you the chance to reflect on and react to anything from feelings to civil war, from hopes to affordable housing. Jennifer, a college senior, says that she likes journal writing because "I am more honest and stronger in my opinions. It has helped me develop a more personal voice in other forms of writing."

Journals are part of almost every student's college writing experience. In many of your courses, you will be required to keep journals. Professors believe that journals play a positive role in both learning and writing. Many colleges and universities believe that teaching writing is the responsibility of the entire faculty, and the journal provides a common vehicle with which to foster writing across the disciplines.

Journals can follow several different formats. In the purest sense, a journal is a diary, a collection of random ideas and reflections captured on paper. "Exploring ideas in writing," explains one professor, "helps students know themselves, which is the first step in discovering a personal style and voice."

Nikki, a college junior from Rhode Island, talks about a bookshelf full of journals that she has maintained for courses and on her own. She speaks of these journals as if they were her friends. Filled, she explains, with doodles and pictures, quotes and notes, the journals have been invaluable to her thinking and writing. She talks about using her journals as sources for writing topics in her nonfiction writing course.

Journals can also have a specific focus. Consider changing your note-taking method to a journal. In your journal, maintain a dialogue with your reading; collect facts, quotations, and other specifics. Also, use the journal to work out ideas on paper; sometimes you may want to do this by jotting notes in the margin. In class, continue the journal format by writing on only one side of the notebook page. Save the adjacent side for your thoughts and reactions. These will generate not only original thoughts and reactions on which to base papers but will force you to interact with the material. Marie, a Macalaster College junior, reflects on how her Russian literature journal was a means of remembering her thoughts and ideas about the reading and class discussions. "I used my journal for collecting quotations to substantiate and develop my essays. I gathered quotes from the reading and jotted down my feelings, reactions, and ideas in the margins for later reference." (A recommended format is provided on page 47.)

Journals offer many side benefits, not the least of which is the motivation to ponder and explore ideas through writing. "I realized that my journal tracked my

Sample Reading/Class Discussion Journal Format

In their purest form, journals do not have a format. A journal closely resembles a diary, and is merely a collection of daily written entries. If, however, you want to develop a new reading and discussion note taking method that will help topic development, documentation, and elaboration, consider the following journal format:

Date of entry: _____

Title of reading: _____

Author: _____

Discussion topic: _____

Quotations/Specifics/Facts (cite sources)

Analysis/Feelings/Comparisons (draw arrows between analysis and specifics)

Pictures/Symbols/Doodles

Vocabulary/Terminology relating to subject and content

Additional comments: keep your thinking current by including quotes and citations from newspaper and/or magazine articles that relate to the subject or theme thoughts and reactions naturally," recalls a student. "It was like a tape recorder of my ideas that I could 'play' over and over again."

A senior from New Mexico discovered a personal writing style emerging in his journals. He explains: "I began to know my style and I finally developed it, so that by my junior year I had become a respectable writer, not just a parrot."

Other students describe their journals as a series of freewrites, letters, lists of facts, brainstormings, and dialogues. Regardless of the format, professors and students agree that journals can improve your reading, thinking, and learning, as well as your writing. You already may have had journal-writing experience. If not, there are lots of books and texts to help you teach yourself this useful skill. (The Recommended Texts section (pages 159–62) lists many good choices.)

Wherever and whenever possible, use a different color ink in your journal to establish a code to facilitate organization for essays or to study for tests and exams. In other words, collect quotes and facts in black ink and use red ink for your analysis. Although this process might appear time-consuming, it will save you endless hours during paper and exam time.

Whenever you pick up a pen or a pencil, you can practice boldness and good writing mechanics. And whenever you read, of course, you can look for models of good writing. Through reading, you can learn grammar, improve vocabulary, develop a personal style, and ensure valid content. Reading and writing go hand-in-hand.

Compositions

Unlike journals, compositions have a public audience—in most cases, your professor. Compositions are a broad term for *focused* writing that presents your personal viewpoint, logically and clearly.

Compositions, like journals, will be part of your writing experience in many disciplines. These assignments broaden your understanding by leading you to investigate ideas and personal experiences through writing. Herein lies the important distinction between compositions and analytical essays. In the words of University of New Hampshire writing instructor Margaret Shirley, "A composition includes your personal feelings on a topic, whereas an analytical essay interprets different texts and points of view on a topic and does not include what you, the writer, feel."

For example, one economics professor asks students to write a composition describing the first time they felt or experienced prejudice. This assignment precedes an examination of the economic forces underlying prejudice that, in turn, precedes a study of the economic factors determining class structure. This professor feels that compositions such as these "enrich students' learning experiences because students are forced to identify with the concept before engaging in a technical study of it."

While there is no universal format for compositions, many students find that the three-part (introduction, body, conclusion) essay model is successful. "Get in and get out," advises a Florida State sophomore. Professors want you to say what you mean to say, illustrate it, and then conclude. They do not want commentary that is vague and drawn out.

Writing compositions can help you understand yourself and the world around you. Realizing that writing can lead to deeper understanding may help you avoid the confusion and frustration of Ellen, a University of Chicago student. Ellen explained to her English professor, "Mr. Williams, I'm trying to get answers and all I get are questions. The margins of my compositions are filled with, 'So what?' or 'What's at stake here?'" The following year,

Ellen wrote in her journal, "Not only did I learn a lot about writing in my composition class, but I also learned about myself."

In a composition on folk crafts, Suzanne, a college junior, probes beyond craftsmanship into areas of human understanding. Her composition on kite making explores the intimate relationship between craftspeople and their crafts. Her last sentence reads: "The quality of making something by hand gives it life and seems to bless it." This composition has moved from the concrete description of colors, fabrics, shapes, and sizes of kites to an abstract philosophical conclusion—the stuff of good college composition writing.

Compositions should make you think and clarify your thoughts. If you select a workable format and then flesh it out with specific, self-reflective illustrations, you are on your way to a good college composition.

Reports

Reports collect, summarize, and then explain data. In physics, for example, a report might explain how microchips work, or in political science, a report might tell us about U.S. immigration patterns during the twentieth century.

One math professor asks his students to write a letter to their grandfathers each week, explaining what they have learned in calculus. This letter becomes an informal report, a chronicle of information, feelings, and perceptions about the events of the week's classes. One rarely thinks of writing in the context of mathematics, but again, colleges are using writing as a way to foster and to evaluate understanding. In grading the letters, the math professor looks for a clear, logical sequence of steps, reporting what has been taught. The degree of clarity and logic, he believes, reflects the degree of understanding.

Most report writing will be more formal than the students' calculus letters to their grandfathers. When asked to write a report in a course, be sure to ask your professor for a format. There are many different guidelines for report writing, and different disciplines favor different formats. In general, however, a report outline breaks down as follows:

1. An overview of the concept or procedure to be reported. In a science report, this would be an explanation of the purpose of the experiment. In a report for a history course, this would be a description of the general background and your position (bias) on the event/concept/phenomenon. Some professors call this an abstract.

2. An enumeration of the specific steps or sequence of events that led to the final outcome(s).

3. A report of the relevant finding(s).

4. A discussion of the final outcome(s).

(Specific formats of science lab reports are profiled in Chapter 5.)

Manuals and stylesheets can help if you are confronted by a report assignment and are not given a format. Even though the professor might ask you to modify your report to meet specific standards, you will have at least an initial outline to guide your writing and a basis for comparison during your revision. These are just two of the benefits of, in the words of one professor, "developing and following a writing method for every assignment you do." This will also allow you to discuss what you have written and how you have written it, and it can help you get off to a focused and organized start.

Research reports generally use a very specific format and they differ from other reports in that you are required to discuss your methodology, materials, and research sources. If you have difficulty locating a stylebook or a format for your report, ask for assistance at the research desk of the college library. Research librarians are trained to help students and to provide you with the information you need.

Analytical Essays

The analytical essay presents a body of documentation to prove a thesis. Consider, for example, the thesis, "Rosa Parks, not Martin Luther King, Jr., began the civil rights movement in the United States." An analytical essay would define the various elements in the statement—Rosa Parks, Martin Luther King, Jr., and the civil rights movement in the United States. Then, the analytical essay would document and analyze Rosa Parks's involvement in the movement to prove that she did indeed begin it.

With few exceptions, students feel that the analytical essay forms the core of college writing. It looms as the giant toward which all college writing is directed. When one considers the 80- to 100-page senior thesis that is part of many college and university writing requirements, one understands why analytical essays remain the number one concern of high school and college students alike. As one college student reports, "You can't get away with anything less than good writing when it comes to analysis. My history professor says that analytical essay writing separates the lightweights from the heavyweights."

A clear format can help you write analytical essays. Stephen describes his writing formula simply: "In my political science courses, I make a statement and then proceed to develop paragraphs that prove why it is true or why it is false." Jessica has a more specific outline for ensuring logic and documentation: "Make statement A and back it up. Make statement B and back it up. Make statement C and back it up." Statements A, B, and C become topic sentences of paragraphs that explore specifics of the thesis statement presented in the introduction. Concluding sentences at the end of every paragraph provide transition and maintain the focus of the thesis. For Jessica, the A, B, C method frames the flow of ideas into a logical sequence. Jessica, a math major, speaks of her method of analysis as an equation: "A + B + C = Thesis."

Several students recommend the "tell them" model, imported from high school, that has stood the test of college writing: "Tell them what you are going to tell them; tell them what you are telling them; tell them what you told them." This simple format provides the structure for an introduction, body, and conclusion. One student reports that she leans on the advice of her professor for developing an analytical essay: "State what you are going to do; state it; and then state it again." For this student, the advice offers a framework that helps her maintain a focus, develop the proof of her argument, and elaborate on the topic.

George Motolanez, a former Russian Studies professor at a selective college, offers this advice for writing an analytical essay: "Make a concise statement. Then, by isolating the subject and predicate of the statement and answering who, what, where, when, and why about each, a focused, organized, and documented analysis unfolds." To understand this approach, take the statement: "Diane Fosse changed our perception of gorillas." You would begin by answering the five W's—who, what, where, when, and why—about Diane Fosse. Then you would apply the same five to the predicate—"changed our perception of gorillas."

When we talked to several of Mr. Motolanez's former students, all agreed that this format works. Dawn, now a sophomore at Amherst College, explains, "After reading my analytical essay out loud to the class, my drama professor asked me to explain my writing process. She said that my essay exemplified not only good writing, but also good thinking. I am eternally grateful to Mr. Motolanez; he saved me from a lot of anxiety and embarrassment, not to mention rewriting."

Essay Tests

In college, as in high school, you will be evaluated in many different ways. Journals, compositions, reports, and analytical essays evaluate your understanding of content material. Certain disciplines incorporate different strategies. Professors of math and economics stress problem sets; natural scientists use multiple-choice and other objective tests; literature professors often spring short-answer reading quizzes; foreign language instructors often rely on dictation. For a majority of courses, however, the essay test dominates.

For many students, the thought of an essay test conjures up an image of frantic hours filling blue examination booklets. "When I have an essay test, I just go in and spill my guts. There just isn't time for anything else," remarks a second-semester freshman. Because professors often criticize essay test writing for being "poorly organized, repetitious, and verbose," it makes sense for you to learn some strategies for taking essay tests.

Peter, a college sophomore, suggests, "It's the time factor, the pressure to perform in one draft that makes essay tests so difficult for me." Ellen, another sophomore, echoes, "My biggest problem is simultaneously having to worry about what I write and how I write. Somehow, I have to prove to the professor that I understand the material, and I have to do it with good writing. It's as if I am taking two tests, a religion test and a writing test."

Before we discuss how to alleviate this anxiety and offer you specific strategies, remember: you must be clear about the writing objective in essay tests. Your goal is to relate precise information about a specific statement or question in an organized and focused fashion.

Strategies for Taking Essay Tests

1. **Anticipate the question.** To do well on essay tests, students advise taking careful notes and listening to professors' hints about what is important. "Nine out of ten times, you can predict an essay question if you take notes carefully and listen," reports a veteran college writer.

2. **Focus.** As soon as you get your test, spend time with the question or statement. First, jot down your gut response to the question. Second, underline the key words and develop a thesis statement using those words. To maintain the focus throughout the essay, list the key words on a piece of scrap paper and brainstorm relevant points and possible answers in columns. If you go blank during the brainstorming process, ask the five W's—who? what? where? when? and why?—for each of the key words. All of the five W's won't apply, but by asking them, you will at least cover all the possible bases and avoid panic at the same time. This will allow you to build a body of specific proof.

3. **Be accurate.** Keep the question in mind, go over your lists looking for irrelevant and superficial information. Add specifics to the brainstorming to in-

sure breadth and depth of discussion. Focus on the task of the question—agree/disagree, compare/contrast, trace/discuss, explain/illustrate—and look for relationships between columns. This will help you expand your discussion of the question beyond the concrete. This step will also help you develop new ideas and relationships instead of just feeding back information from the course readings and discussions.

4. **Write an outline and response.** Use the lists and established relationships you discovered in step 3 to sketch a rough outline and then write a response.

5. **Go over the draft.** Ask yourself the following: Have I answered all questions? Have I included enough specific facts? Have I analyzed the facts to show relationships and significance?

6. **Check your spelling.** Content is important in essay tests; a professor is likely to be convinced that you know the material if names and terms are spelled correctly. One student turned red as she related the story of misspelling *Ghandi* throughout an essay test in world history. She said that the C+ grade she received reflected her carelessness. To avoid this, students recommend paying close attention to spelling when preparing for essay tests. The names and any specific language or terms of the course must be spelled correctly. One way to do this is to keep a list of terms (perhaps in your journal) and to review the spelling of these terms for a few minutes each day.

7. **Remember the Big Seven.** Keep a mental checklist of the seven elements of good writing discussed in Chapter 2. You might even jot them down on the top of your test.

8. **Organize your time.** Divide your allotted time into three parts: brainstorming and outlining, writing,

and checking for errors and revising. This will allow
you to establish the best conditions for not only demonstrating your knowledge and understanding of the
material but also for presenting it clearly, logically,
and accurately.

9. **Make these steps habit.** Practice these steps regardless of whether you have 20 minutes or 3 hours or
   whether you are writing a one paragraph or a five-
   page response. A writing strategy can make the difference. Practice good writing habits out of class
   when writing analytical essays. These habits will
   carry over to in-class writing situations.

Risk Taking in Essay Tests

A group of older students, especially those in the humanities and social sciences, report writing creative responses to essay tests. They spin off the question rather
than just feed back information. They feel that essay tests
offer merely another forum for demonstrating knowledge,
and that it is the writer's prerogative to present the facts
creatively. Bill tells of answering a question about the
Lincoln/Douglas debates in letter form, with Douglas writing Lincoln in a final appeal. Bill reports a positive reaction from his professor. "I followed all the rules of logic
and documentation. I feel that my writing was clearer
because I had clearly defined my point of view (Douglas)
and my audience (Lincoln)." The veterans, however, warn
that it is important to know your professor before making
a radical format change. These same students feel that this
is important no matter what. If the professors are your
primary writing audience, you need to invest time in getting to know them.

Conclusion

At times, you might feel overwhelmed by the different demands of college writing. It is important, however, to realize that all the writing you do, no matter what the form, strengthens your writing skills.

1. **Journal writing** strengthens your writing voice and personal style. Ideas and questions that you may want to pursue can also emerge from journals. Remember, developing creative topics is an essential skill of a good writer.

2. **Compositions** will be part of your writing in many disciplines, and they offer you the chance to strengthen all of the elements outlined in Chapter 2.

3. **Report writing,** presenting and understanding the information, is a first step before you explore the why's of analysis.

4. **Analytical essays** demand focus, logic and clarity, and elaboration.

5. **Essay tests** are merely a shortened and timed version of analytical essays.

Writing
for the
Disciplines

"It took me a while to understand that even though content differed among my courses, there was a common requirement for clear, logical, substantiated writing. At first, confusion reigned, and I felt that each professor wanted something different. Once I calmed down and found the common writing bond among my courses, I could attack different writing assignments confidently," comments Louisa, a senior, reflecting on her college writing experience.

When professors ask for good writing, no matter what the area of study, they want nothing less than good thinking. Professors want your writing to be clear and precise. A professor from a small southern college offers this perspective, "I always tell my students that you might never write a science lab report or music history paper again. You will, however, have to write clearly and persuasively for a variety of audiences for the rest of your life." When you write in a foreign language, follow the same advice you would for a science lab report or a history paper: stick to the Big Seven. A sociology and an electrical engineering paper both depend on logic, and diction is just as important in writing for religion as it is for ecology.

Although there are some writing conventions for different disciplines, definitions of good writing within areas of study are far more similar than dissimilar. This chapter reaffirms the point that writing is important in college no matter what you study. It focuses on five different disciplines in order to give you insight into the writing experiences in each area.

To give you an idea of the different subjects generally taught within each discipline, a representative listing follows.

Social Sciences: anthropology, government, history*, political science, sociology

Natural Sciences: biology, chemistry, geology, physics

Humanities: art, English, philosophy, music, theater

Foreign Languages: Arabic, Chinese, French, German, Hebrew, Russian, Spanish

Business and Technology: accounting, computer science, finance, engineering

Certain guidelines within each discipline can help you direct your writing. Perhaps the most pronounced difference in writing among the disciplines is audience. Gary, an accounting major, tells us "to write for an auditor," while Carlos believes that his English professors "want writers to capture their attention." Once you know the demands of the different disciplines, you will be better able to evaluate your own writing. Knowing these criteria will help you figure out what a political science, chemistry, or engineering professor wants. Keep in mind that though there are differences, the definition of good writing for one subject usually fits other academic areas as well.

Social Sciences

In your social science courses, professors will ask for straightforward, expository writing. Martha, a political science major, observes, "Professors assign writing in which the goal is to answer questions, define terms, and

---

* History can be in either social sciences or humanities; in this chapter, it is included under the former.

explain causes and effects." Assignments that ask *what, why, how,* and *if* will provide focus for your writing.

John McCardell, a history professor at Middlebury College, explains, "I care about how well a student can explain a historical term or situation and how a student can analyze, using evidence. To do this well requires familiarity with the material and the ability to address the problem simply and logically using the available evidence. History students must realize that before they can interpret or analyze, or before they can condemn or praise, they must understand; only then can they make the reader understand."

For Professor McCardell and many of his colleagues, social science writing asks you to:

- Define terms.

- Explain situations.

- Analyze your terms and/or situations.

- Support your ideas with specific evidence.

- Present your analysis and evidence.

- Make the reader understand the terms and/or situations.

- Demonstrate understanding through writing.

As part of a European history class, you might be asked to write a one-page response to a book, question, or discussion topic each week. Weekly writing drills such as this offer practice in good writing and support clear thinking and articulation during class discussion. For example, after reading a book on Trotsky, your assignment might be to discuss how an aspect of his life affected his view of the world, as Molly did in the first two paragraphs of the following paper.

Trotsky's life was typical of a rural middle-class family, but, looking back, it is easy to see how the events of his early life shaped his later philosophy. His emotionless family life, his brilliant but tarnished school career, and his outstanding intelligence and inquisitiveness are all clues to understanding Trotsky's later life.

Trotsky's home life was reasonably happy but not exceedingly so. Although his father became successful, Trotsky was raised frugally. He said, "We knew no need but neither did we know the generosities of life." His parents were hard-working people and did not pay much attention to their children. Trotsky was often left to his own devices and spent his time with his parents' servants. It is here that his indignation at the condition of the common people grew. When discussing a poor woman who walked seven versts to collect one ruble, he said, "It made my heart tighten to look at that figure—the embodiment of poverty and submission." It was this compassion and the ability to control his emotions that allowed Trotsky to become a revolutionary leader.

The comment on Molly's paper (which got an A), "Good job of limiting the scope of your analysis," reveals another writing criterion of the social sciences. Professors want you to establish a specific focus and examine it in depth, rather than present a general discussion of a broad topic. The small red dot at the end of each line of Molly's graded paper indicates that her professor was searching for a logical sequence of ideas that were clearly stated and substantiated.

What has Molly done to merit the praise "good job"? From the start, she limits the scope of her analysis by looking at the impact of Trotsky's early life on his later philosophy.

Recognizing the general nature of the opening statement, Molly further narrows her discussion in the next sentence, which becomes the thesis of the essay. "His emotionless family life, his brilliant but tarnished school career, and his outstanding intelligence and inquisitiveness are all clues to understanding Trotsky's later life." This three point statement elaborates upon the first sentence and provides organization and content for the rest of the paper. The topic sentences that follow and the substantiating details indicate that Molly understood her thesis and could discuss her idea in depth.

The logical sequence of the topic sentences lends clear structure to the essay. This is so important that professors in several disciplines, including foreign languages and the natural sciences, urge students to write a topic sentence outline—either *before* writing the essay, in order to provide logic, or *after*, to test the logic of your argument.

Molly's essay illustrates another important criterion of social science writing: terse analysis. The assignment required one page of writing that was based on several hundred pages of reading, challenging the myth that good college writing means long papers. Indeed, many history professors require that freshmen limit themselves to between four and eight paragraphs per assignment to state and defend their arguments.

Because they want you to make your meaning clear, social science professors often allow revisions. One student explains, "In my history courses, more than any other, I rely on my circle of writing friends to question me about what I mean and what I have written. My professor is constantly asking us to look at not only what we have written but how we have written it. She wants us to choose precise words."

Clear, direct prose requires that your written work be free of the mechanical errors described in Chapter 2. Many social scientists urge students to have grammar handbooks with them whenever they are writing. To help freshmen produce writing assignments that are polished and error-free, professors often incorporate time for rewriting. When we looked at several freshman sociology, history, and political science syllabuses, we found not only weekly writing assignments but revisions and rewrites of previously assigned papers. Your writing assignment for one week could be to rewrite a previous assignment. You will find professors using this practice in the other disciplines, as well.

"Even though my professors are sticklers about a tightly written essay, they still want creativity," observes Elyse, a sophomore history major. Social science professors encourage creativity and a personal voice. You might, for example, be given an assignment like this one, given to members of a class on Great Thinkers, at a small Maine college: "Darwin, Dostoevsky, and Skinner meet for tea, and you are lucky enough to be invited. Discussion naturally turns to the evolution of humankind. Record the discussion." While this assignment differs from the essay, the criteria of focus, logic, depth, and substantiation remain unchanged. With an assignment like this one, you can assume a personal, involved voice. In Chapter 9 you will discover how some students are experimenting with this challenge.

Natural Sciences

Natural scientists believe that their audience separates them from other writers. Alyssia, a bio-chem major, discusses the importance of audience: "We approach our lab reports as if they are to be published in scientific journals." Accuracy is emphasized; there is no room for flowery language. A fellow scientist should be able to duplicate your experiment, using the same materials and following the exact process outlined in your report, and then compare and contrast outcomes.

One of the components of natural science writing is the structural formula. Almost all lab reports, whether technical or scientific, follow this format: title, abstract (a

100- to-200-word summary of the project), introduction, methods and materials, results, discussion and conclusion, and references. Articles in professional journals often follow this format as well.

Does this sound familiar? It most likely resembles your high school biology, chemistry, or physics lab write-ups. College lab write-ups, however, demand specific details about equipment (brand names), methods and procedures (enough information to allow replication of the experiment), and detailed discussion (proof that you both understand and can interpret the experiment). Most colleges and universities offer a stylesheet for these reports; be sure to ask your professor for specific guidelines.

Randy Landgren, former chairperson of Middlebury's natural science division, recommends to his students the following writing plan for papers of five or more pages. Although the formula is intended for the natural sciences, it works with other disciplines as well.

- Choose a topic.

- Become more informed about that topic.

- Hone the topic until it fits your goal (limit your focus).

- Write an outline that defines the flow of your paper.

- Write a topic-sentence outline that defines each of the paragraphs that will be found in your final paper.

- Write the paragraphs.

- Refine your topic-sentence outline.

- Check transitions to see that your proposed flow has not been violated.

- Check paragraphs to see that your topic-sentence outline has not been lost.

- Share the results with friends, professors, or a peer tutor.

- Proofread for mechanics.

- Revise.

- Revise.

- Revise.

Although this process may read like a recipe, good writers in any discipline develop a writing formula that suits their needs. The call for logic and order in the topic-sentence outline mirrors the writing objective explained by the social scientists.

Your science professors might ask you to be creative by encouraging journal writing. Students in the natural sciences may use journals to record personal thoughts on chemical structures or on the global impact of physics. Eventually, they share these thoughts or incorporate them into a formal essay. A geology professor might ask you to write a composition answering the questions: What is time? How do humans conceive time? How does the earth reflect time? This assignment, explains the professor, is "more an exercise in ideas than in an understanding of glacial movement and geological principles." Notice, however, that the three-point assignment offers an outline for an introduction, body, and conclusion. This structure leads to focus, logic, and elaboration.

Below are two paragraphs of a report that Kim, a sophomore, wrote for an introductory biology course.

An earthworm is a more complex organism than a flatworm. While an earthworm possesses a closed circulatory system including hearts and blood vessels, a flatworm has none. The flatworm's cells are within diffusion distance of a food source. The earthworm's flow-through digestive system is also more complex than the flatworm's with its one opening. The earthworm's excretion is carried out by nephridia, while the flatworm excretes its waste by purging and using flame cells. The nervous system of the earthworm consists of nerve cords originating at a cerebral ganglion (primitive brain), while flatworms possess either a nerve net or small nerve cords. In addition, the segmented earthworm has a complex muscle system while the unsegmented flatworm depends upon simple muscle cells and cilia.

The superior structure of the earthworm's body allows it to function with more complexity than the flatworm. The earthworm, due to its circulation, can gain nutrients through digestion only and can tolerate a wider variation in environment than the flatworm, which must keep its cells close to nourishment. The earthworm's more sophisticated nervous system enables it to sense and respond to stimuli like moisture, light, and touch, but the flatworm has only limited sensory capabilities. Also, the muscular segments, which are capable of peristaltic action, allow the earthworm a much broader range of motion.

Kim's report gets off to a good start. Good science writers, like social scientists, recommend that you first state your idea clearly. The first sentence of Kim's paper establishes the focus "An earthworm is a more complex organism than a flatworm."

Kim then develops this idea with logical conclusions and elaboration supported by data. The earthworm is more complex because it has "a closed circulatory system including hearts and blood vessels," a "flow-through digestive system," and so on. Development requires simple short sentences that are unencumbered by modifiers and prepositional phrases. Maggie O'Brien, a bio-chem professor, notes, "There should always be a little voice whispering, 'Be concise, make it shorter, make it shorter.' "

Humanities

"In humanities classes, the only thing that really changes is the subject of my writing," claims Brooke, a Dartmouth senior. In literature courses, assigned essays often ask you to discuss themes, imagery, personification, diction, voice, tone, mood, character development, and setting; you might do this in a short story, novel, or poem. Requiring close textual analysis, the writing demands focus, clarity, logic, and specific documentation.

A music major from a small midwestern college writes, "In a paper on American music, I discussed how in Virgil Thomson's 1930s suite *The Plow That Broke the Plains* the music evoked certain imagery. This assignment wasn't any different from those in my literature classes that asked me to analyze, discuss, compare, and contrast."

Instead of a story or a poem, in an art history assignment your writing would focus on a painting or sculpture. You might be asked to brainstorm and then write about the details of color, style, lighting, or symbolism. Or, you might be asked to discuss a theme in several works of art. An art history professor at a southern university describes an assignment in which he asks students to examine the theme of anxiety in a series of modern paintings. You would need to make a specific statement about anxiety, and then construct a series of paragraphs to illustrate your thesis. When presenting your substantiating details, you would make a *link* between the details of the painting and the feeling of anxiety—in other words, *analyze*.

"My religion professor taught me how to write," claims Joel, a sophomore from Ohio. "She told us to omit introductions and get to the heart of our writing, and she insisted that our essays should have three parts: a lead, a middle, and an end." Good writing, according to Joel's professor, is filled with specific references to the readings and few references to personal opinions and feelings. Therefore, to analyze Buddhist philosophy, you would focus on a specific text, not write what you feel about Buddhist ideology. This advice was so important to Joel's writing that he taped it above his desk.

Humanities professors look for bold, creative topics and voices. In a discussion about favorite writing assign-

ments, Karen, an English major from the University of
Michigan, glows as she describes a recent writing exercise.
Karen had presented the character of Humbert from Na-
bokov's *Lolita* using lyrics. Parodying Simon and Garfun-
kel's "Cecilia," Karen follows the rules of effective writing
in the following excerpt. A clear, logical presentation, using carefully selected words, delivers a bold, creative por-
trayal:

> Desolation,
> She loves someone else,
> She's used me and thrown me away.
>
> Consolation,
> He won't have her long,
> I'll shoot him and blow him away.

In a more traditional, but equally provocative way,
Peter, a sophomore from Ithaca College, examined the
character of Huckleberry Finn in a paper entitled, "Voices
of the Sea." Recognized for its freshness, Peter's title drew
positive marks for cleverness from his professor. She was
"tempted by the title from the start, finding it playful and
original." Peter continued his boldness by beginning his
paper with a quotation about the sea from another novel,
The Awakening. Suddenly, Huck's rebirth and transforma-
tion evolved from the "seductive and sensuous" quality of
the sea. Peter now had a fresh focus and rich language for
his essay.

Foreign Languages

When Professor Judith Liskin-Gasparro of Middlebury's Spanish Department talks about good writing in
foreign languages, she echoes the prescription for good
writing in the other disciplines. "Clear, accurate, and per-
suasive" head her list.

71

In some ways, however, foreign language writing is different. It can be frustrating to try to convey a 19-year-old's thoughts with what is often a 6-year-old's vocabulary. This limited vocabulary, comments Professor Liskin-Gasparro, can be "an asset, not a liability." A limited vocabulary forces you to "get down to basics and rely on organization and structure." In foreign languages, you have to get to the point directly. You cannot hide behind "page-long preambles or flowery prose," explains a professor of Soviet Studies. A student of German agrees: "With a limited vocabulary and even more limited exposure to writing in German, I held onto structure for dear life. I appreciated my high school training in the five-paragraph essay."

Nevertheless, foreign language professors urge students to avoid turning writing into grammar and spelling exercises. When this happens, you stop being bold. Your thinking becomes constricted, and you are unable to use writing to explore your thoughts. "In my first-year Spanish course, I did my freewriting in English. In this way I kept my writing idea-oriented and not grammar-oriented. Now that I have a broader vocabulary and am more proficient in the language, I freewrite mostly in Spanish. Because spelling and mechanics don't matter in freewriting, I take greater risks with the language. When I revise I feel challenged to explore new vocabulary and grammar," explains Maya, a sophomore at a Texas college. "This helps students think in the second language rather than just translate from their first language," adds a foreign language professor.

Because most introductory courses rely on written exercises to teach sentence structure, it is easy to forget good writing habits in a new language.

Many of the steps that produce good writing in English also lead to good foreign language writing. As you develop proficiency, remember the Big Seven. Transfer your personal writing process to your foreign language writing. Professors in upper-level courses use brainstorming, freewriting, and journal writing to build confidence in students. An Indiana University professor recommends a four-step process for writing in a foreign language.

Step 1. Prewrite on a topic. Freewrite, then discuss in student groups, and finally develop a sequence of topic sentences that outline your position.

Step 2. Draft an essay of 250 words or less on the topic.

Step 3. Revise and edit. Meet in both small and large groups to ask each other: "Does this make sense to you?" "Do my paragraphs follow a logical order?" "Is this the correct use of this word?"

Step 4. Write your final draft.

This four-step process offers weekly writing practice for elementary foreign language students. During the initial two sessions (steps 1 and 2 occur in week one, steps 3 and 4, in week two), students produce "coherent, grammatical, descriptive, analytical prose." The writing assignments assume many forms: summaries of current articles from *Time* and *Newsweek*, analyses of characters in contemporary short stories, and compare/contrast analytical essays. Beyond encouraging good writing habits, these activities help students to begin thinking in the language, a necessary step to fluency.

Here are some recommendations designed to help you become a good foreign language writer:

- **Develop a reading regimen.** Make sure it includes newspapers and magazines in the foreign language. Reading will expand your vocabulary and heighten your awareness of sentence structure.

- **Learn to word process in the language.** Word processing programs are available in almost every language.

- **Use a dictionary.** Careful cross-referencing of words to discover correct usage is an important step to take in becoming a good foreign-language writer. Accurate diction and an extended vocabulary are key elements of good writing.

- **Immerse yourself.** Your new language needs to become natural. Radio and television news and soap operas are available to you in foreign languages via satellite, or in some areas, cable.

- **Take risks.** Whenever possible, write on topics of interest. This will help motivate you to explore new vocabulary and sentence structure.

Business and Technology

Demands and approach make business and technology kindred disciplines. Good writing in the business and technical fields, not surprisingly, is similar to that in other disciplines, and emphasizes the Big Seven.

Writing in business and technical fields uses formats such as memorandums, letters, and reports. Business and technical writing most resembles the analytical essay because it is formal, focused writing that requires both documentation and analysis. Business and technical writing also stresses a defined voice and demands word economy.

If you've heard the saying "Time is money," you'll understand why professors from the business and technical fields emphasize brevity. You'll want to avoid personal feelings or unsupported projections. Don't write, as did one freshman business major, "It's my feeling that profit margins are related to astrological forces, although this is difficult to prove." As David, a business major at Northeastern explains, "Professors constantly remind us that key decisions worth millions of dollars ride on our ability to write clearly."

Business and technical writing demands concrete, specific language. One student advises: "Don't use words that could never come out of your mouth. Use words you know." Always find the clearest word possible; for example: *begin* for *commence, use* for *utilize.* You need to find one word to take the place of several; for example, *simultaneously* replaces *at the same time; many indications* replaces *there were many indications.* To be accessible to both the layperson and the professional, your language must be clear and precise. Your key points must not be obscured by unnecessary detail. Indeed, you should practice this in all disciplines.

Unlike writing in the humanities, social sciences, and foreign languages, but as in the natural sciences, business and technical writing most often follows specific formats. Learn which formats are acceptable and follow them. When in doubt, ask your professor to outline the preferred format.

During your freshman and sophomore years in technical disciplines, you will devote between 15 and 30 percent of your academic time to writing. When you are a junior and senior, that percentage will increase. At Rensselaer Polytechnic Institute, for example, the senior engineering project demands sophisticated research and writing skills. The project also requires students to bring drafts of their writing to the RPI Writing Center, where, according to its director Karen LeFevre, they are taught to write in a way that promotes clear thinking. Important steps include brainstorming, freewriting, drafting, revising, and editing.

If you pursue electrical engineering, you probably will have to write a thesis similar to RPI's. The RPI guidelines below summarize the format of effective technical writing:

- A one- or two-sentence introduction, summarizing the project and explaining why you are proposing it."

  Scientists, engineers, and business people are deluged with reports and memos. They must be able to absorb the material quickly and easily.

- In the body of your proposal, use headings to indicate separate sections."

  Clarity is achieved through structure, organization, diction, and visual presentation. You need to order material so that it reads easily. Headings, highlighted key points, tables, and graphs all serve as sign posts, allowing your reader to know where he or she is at a glance.

- Reports need to be intelligible not only to an immediate supervisor but also to corporate executives.

In a business course, a professor might ask you to assume the role of a loan officer, corporate manager, or financier and to write a case study or a business memorandum. This would force you to identify with a real situation and to make decisions. Get to the point from the start. Present the problem and procedure; do not distract your reader with digressions. Information is only important if it is part of either the solution or the product.

Megan's memorandum to a bank manager suggests a format that you can follow in your business writing.

- **Present the problem.** The thesis statement presents the focus of your memo ("The recent slowdown in teller transactions"), which leads to the recommendations or conclusions you draw.

- **Summarize the situation.** Offer the present conditions and relevant background information that frame the problem.

TO: Bank Manager
FROM: Megan Laslocky, Assistant Manager
SUBJECT: Teller Transactions
DATE: February 22, 1989

The recent slowdown in teller transactions indicates that our tellers have not mastered the new computer system.

Two months ago we implemented a new software system to speed up teller transactions. Instead of 21 transactions per hour (the 1984–1988 rate), we are down to 17 transactions per hour over the last two months.

This slowdown is costing the bank money: the cost per transaction is now $.92, compared to the previous cost of $.76, and we are losing customers frustrated by longer lines.

I recommend that tellers attend the two-hour training session on the new software system that will take place this Thursday between 3:30 and 5:30 p.m. Bill Jenkins of Software Sales will teach the session. Please let me hear from you by tomorrow.

- **Analyze the central problem, make recommendations, and offer a solution.** Solutions should follow a logical plan. The central problem in this example is the slowdown in teller transactions; the recommendation is that the tellers have a training session to improve their use of the software.

- **Evaluate the report for clarity.** Discard unnecessary information and details, so that analysis and recommendations are concise and sequential. Ask yourself: Have I used precise words? Have I written in the active voice? Are my recommendations assertive and purposeful?

Clare Corcoran, a recent Harvard graduate who is currently a loan officer at a Florida bank, notes that, "Business writing is the nuclear meltdown of ideas."

Conclusion

Although the amount of writing you will do in college is related to subject area—humanities courses generally require more writing than those in engineering and business—writing is important in all disciplines. Clearly, good writers have an advantage in college, no matter what subjects they pursue. Good writing skills are also an asset in virtually all professions and careers.

The different writing expectations of each discipline are a function of audience. You need to keep in mind for whom you are writing. The professor of humanities is concerned with voice and creativity; of the social sciences, with logic and elaboration; of the natural sciences, with precision and conciseness; of foreign languages, with authenticity and structure; of business and technology, with form and precision.

Preparing in High School for College Writing

"**A**s I packed the car, I didn't know what to expect—new roommate, new food, early field hockey. Writing my first college paper was the furthest thing from my mind. In retrospect, I wish that this had not been the case. In fact, I keep wondering why I didn't spend more time working on my writing in high school. I had so many opportunities to talk with teachers and work on my writing skills, but I was always so afraid of failure, so defensive about my writing that I stayed away. The last thing I wanted to do was rewrite my essay," confesses Myra, a sophomore from Indiana.

Myra's feeling that she is unprepared for college writing is not unusual. Realizing that she could have done more to prepare is also common. What Myra and many students do not realize is that there are many ways to practice and improve writing during high school. Because you will find yourself writing no matter where you go to college or what program you pursue, it makes sense to spend some time researching precollege writing possibilities.

This chapter offers suggestions about ways you can take charge of your writing while still in high school—steps that will at least minimize, if not eliminate writing anxiety. Not so long ago, preparing for college writing meant drills in grammar and composition. But now writing has become an opportunity to explore, to make new friends, and to work closely with a high school teacher. To help you develop a plan to prepare for college writing, you might want to begin with the self-assessments that follow.

Professors say that you are a good writer if you know yourself. When asked to define this self-knowledge, a professor from a small southern college commented, "Self-knowing writers recognize weaknesses and strengths, do not fear criticism, and have developed a personal writing plan." To begin the self-discovery process, you'll need to ask yourself some questions. Below is an exercise to help you get started.

Writing Self-Assessment I

	Y	N
1. I am writing every day.	☐	☐
2. I am writing essays in class that are at least one page.	☐	☐
3. I am writing essays outside of class that are at least one page.	☐	☐
4. I am writing in my English class.	☐	☐
5. I am writing in my social studies or history class.	☐	☐
6. I have a friend or parent read my papers.	☐	☐
7. I go over my papers after they are handed back and try to understand the teachers' comments.	☐	☐
8. I ask teachers to go over my essays to help me understand my writing strengths and weaknesses.	☐	☐
9. I rewrite my papers when it is necesary.	☐	☐
10. I practice journal writing.	☐	☐
11. I read every day.	☐	☐

If you are able to answer "yes" to most of these statements, you are well on your way to becoming a good college writer. You are actively engaged in writing; you aren't afraid of criticism; you are taking responsibility for your development as a writer.

Step 1. If you are unable to answer "yes" to most of the above statements, consider turning them into tasks for your "writing action plan." Take on a few of these as personal challenges so that before you enter college, you can answer "yes" more than you answer "no." Here are three suggestions to help you write more frequently and more effectively.

- **Start a journal so that you write two or three times a week.** Write a page or two about books, movies, friends, school, family, anger, embarrassment, or love. It doesn't matter what you write about, but whether you put pen to paper. Also, try using the journal format provided at the end of Chapter 4 in your history, science, or English class. Practicing these new writing methods will help you when you are on your own in college.

- **Have a friend read one of your essays and react to just its content.** All writing assessments don't have to involve grammar and spelling. Use your friend as a sounding board for your ideas. Have your friend indicate areas of confusion with a question mark to help you test your writing for logic and clarity. One high school teacher asks her students to respond to a friend's paper with a compliment, a question, and a recommended change. Ask one of your friends to do the same.

- **Ask a teacher to help you with one of your writing assignments.** Go with specific questions rather than a general plea for help. Ask for assistance in revising an awkward sentence or in developing a thesis. Teachers are busy, but most will make time to work with students who have specific needs and want to improve their writing.

83

Step 2. Once you are comfortable with criticism and once writing becomes habitual, you can begin a comprehensive personal writing evaluation. Review the list of effective writing characteristics outlined in Chapter 2 and then respond to the statements in Self-Assessment II.

Writing Self-Assessment II

	Y	N
1. I am familiar with five or more of the Big Seven: Logic, Clarity, Diction, Audience, Boldness, Elaboration, Mechanics.	☐	☐
2. I can use these terms to talk about my writing.	☐	☐
3. I have friends who understand these terms and with whom I share and/or confer about my writing.	☐	☐
4. I have teachers evaluate my writing using these criteria of effective writing.	☐	☐
5. I have a writing process that includes pre-writing, drafting, and revising.	☐	☐
6. When I read, I look for and collect models of good writing.	☐	☐

If you can answer "yes" to four or more of the questions in Writing Self-Assessment II, the transition to college writing should be smooth. If your high school does not offer a support network of friends and faculty, go to your school or public library or local bookstore and locate one of the books listed in the bibliography. If they are unavailable, ask your school librarian to purchase some of the recommended writing texts and begin a writing library. Many of these books offer practice drills, and one that is especially helpful is *Writing Without Teachers* by Peter Elbow.

Step 3. Before you get to college, know the writing requirements, offerings, and support services of the institution you plan to attend. The self-assessments can help you identify your writing strengths and weaknesses and thus determine your writing needs.

Some colleges either urge or require you to take a semester or two of writing courses. Others require you to take a writing-intensive seminar if your SAT scores are below a certain point. At Colgate University, you might spend the summer before your freshman year corresponding with a professor both to describe yourself as a writer and to convey what kinds of college writing instruction you would like to have.

Knowing what course requirements and writing demands to expect in college will place you in an advantageous position: it will increase the chance of a successful match between you and your college and will reduce the number of surprises once you get there.

Preparing during the Academic Year

For some students, the writing demands of their high school courses are rigorous enough for them to feel prepared for college writing. Because the number one recommendation of professors and students is to write as much as you can in high school, you need to make an honest assessment of your writing skills.

If the writing self-assessments reveal that you are not writing enough in classes, find ways to increase your writing time. Consider keeping either course or personal journals. Journals promote good thinking and writing. Use the course journal format provided in Chapter 4 or freewrite in your diary. At the end of each day, go over your class notes and select an idea that dominated a good part of the discussion. Or, while you are reading for the next class, select an important topic. For example, from your psychology reading choose Erikson's theory about adolescent identity confusion. Following the rules of freewriting outlined in Chapter 3, write as much as you can about your own adolescence in order to discover if and when you have experienced this sort of identity confusion. Or, select a quotation from a short story. Copy it in your notebook and then write for several minutes, or until you have filled a page, about the character or idea of the passage. Remember, as one student describes it, freewriting is "thinking and talking on paper."

When you freewrite in a course journal, you practice "focused" freewriting. Instead of letting your mind wander, you keep your thoughts directed to the topic and freewrite to explore the idea. Topics for further class discussion or for compositions and essays evolve from focused freewriting. Focused freewriting serves a dual purpose. First, it builds your confidence as a writer, and second, it encourages critical thinking through writing. (Chapter 9 will explain how these freewrites can also strengthen your voice and style.)

If you feel the need to beef up your writing regimen, see if your high school offers writing electives in journalism or expository or creative writing. Supplement your regular English course with these electives in your junior or senior year. But don't take these electives in place of a literature course, for, as many professors note, "Good reading and good writing go hand-in-hand." You can improve your writing by reading and vice versa.

Even if the writing demands of your academic program are sufficient, consider extracurricular options for writing.

1. Write for your school newspapers and literary magazines. These excellent writing outlets will help you hone your skills and challenge you to use the Big Seven. You will have the experience of writing for a public audience rather than a private one (a teacher), and you will also build a peer support group of other writers. The more steps you take to make writing part of your daily routine, the greater your chances are of being prepared when you get to college.

2. Join your high school debate team. Debating develops all seven areas of effective writing outlined in Chapter 2. If you debate, for example, the issue whether or not the United States government should subsidize private education, you hone different writing-related skills. These include persuasion, argumentation, and clear and logical thinking. In a debate, you must take a position and then support it logically and specifically. You cannot avoid using the opposing point of view in your argument; doing so will help you gain valuable practice in developing complex thesis statements. You also gain important experience in working with a live audience.

3. Form a writing club, an informal group of friends who get together regularly and share their writing. Charlene, a senior at a New Jersey high school, explains that her writing club grew out of a sophomore composition class. "We had to have a conference with a friend after each draft we wrote. After doing this for a semester, a group of us couldn't imagine getting through Advanced Placement without one another. Then we began meeting evenings to read aloud our essays, reports, and poems and to make suggestions that would make our writing more effective. When we couldn't meet, we would exchange papers and write responses. It made writing less lonely."

4. Participate in writing contests. Many colleges, universities, states, and community and national organizations, including the National Council of Teachers of English, sponsor writing contests throughout the year. Offering a discerning audience (other than teachers) and a reason to write (other than for grades), contests challenge your writing effectiveness in fiction, nonfiction, poetry, essays, short stories, and personal-opinion pieces. To find out about their availability, contact your principal, the heads of your social studies, history, or English departments, or your guidance counselor. Don't wait for them to distribute information. Be aggressive and go after them. You can also write your state department of education. The English consultant should be able to mail a list of writing contests to you.

5. Write letters to the editor and to your local newspaper and state legislators. Authentic writing experiences give you important practice in clear, concise writing. When you care about issues, you are more likely to be bold. You might even want to try a few of these in your writing group, in a social studies class, or on your own.

In short, seize every possible opportunity to practice your writing. Nowhere is the maxim "Practice makes perfect" truer than in writing.

Preparing during the Summer

Raul, a high school senior, strengthened his writing skills before college. "At the Governor's Institute, I worked with professional writers; this changed the way I felt about my writing and about myself as a writer. In high school I was never given the opportunity to write for a real audience, to see my writing in print, or to discuss my writing as an equal."

Summer writing opportunities abound. Increasingly, colleges are opening their campuses to high school students by sponsoring summer writing programs. Following a workshop format, student writers of fiction, poetry, and nonfiction spend from one to six weeks working with professionals in the writing field. Vermont's Bennington College is one of the many places offering a summer conference for high school students.

There are also summer programs that are more technically oriented. Georgetown University, for instance, hosts a program that brings together high school students to sharpen their science- and technical-writing skills. The program also teaches the rudiments of science research writing.

If you are interested in pursuing these opportunities, contact the English departments at nearby colleges to inquire about writing programs and institutes. Your state department of education may have a directory of summer writing programs. Teachers and guidance counselors may also be able to help, though it is impossible for them to know about all of the available options. *You* need to take charge of your writing development. These programs can make the difference in your writing preparation for college; your effort will not be wasted.

Developing Word-Processing Skills

Many colleges offer a crash course in word processing during freshman orientation. James, a student from Colorado, insists, "It saved my life." Several college peer tutors who train freshmen in word processing advise high school students to learn the fundamentals of word processing *before* college. Remy, a sophomore from Florida, admits to having avoided the computer in high school because he didn't know how to type. "If I had it to do over again," Remy claims, "I'd make keyboarding and word-processing skills my top priority while getting ready for college."

Many students don't have the opportunity to work with computers and learn word processing in high school. As Martina comments, "I never touched a computer keyboard until I went to college. I was scared, but it was a matter of survival. Unless I wanted to pay a fortune to have someone else type my papers, I had to learn how to word process."

If you have the opportunity to learn before you get to college, you will save yourself time and money. How can you get ready?

1. Learn how to type, or at least learn your way around a keyboard. All typewriters and computers have the same basic arrangement; when there are differences, they are minor. When you get to college, you can take time to learn the particulars of your college's system.

   Keyboarding computer programs can help with this process. Sometimes called "typing tutors," these programs teach letter and symbol location by projecting a keyboard on the screen. One such program is "Mavis Beacon Teaches Typing."

2. If word processing is not part of your high school's curriculum, check vocational/technical high schools or community colleges in your area for evening or summer courses. Many word-processing courses are taught in conjunction with keyboarding.

   If your high school has a computer center, visit it and ask the staff for a word-processing program and instructions. Most beginning programs can be self-administered by merely following the commands that appear on the screen. Try to visit the center on a regular basis. Begin typing your papers on the computer or type messages or letters. Better yet, begin a journal. When you have time, make a new entry. You will then be developing three important writing skills: keyboarding, word processing, and journal writing.

3. As soon as you know what college or university you are going to attend, find out what computers they use. Macintosh and IBM are now the most popular on college campuses. If at all possible, train yourself to use that hardware and appropriate software. The summer before you enter college, make this a priority. Keep in mind that once you are familiar with one system, it is easy to pick up another.

7

College Support Systems for Writing

"Most of my high school teachers are willing to go over my rough drafts with me. Can I expect this in college?" Dozens of high school seniors with whom we spoke wondered the same thing. Of course, the answers to a question like this will vary, depending on the college or professor, but most colleges do assist in your transition to college writing and create supports to sustain your writing throughout your four years.

Some of the high school students we interviewed were not concerned about writing support services. Frank, a high school senior, offers this brave philosophy, "To me, writing, like the whole college experience, is a challenge. I figure, it's my job to adapt and succeed. That's why I'm going to a large midwestern university. I want to test myself."

If you are like the majority of high school students, however, you have questions about writing support. This chapter discusses how to find that writing support; what, specifically, you can expect; and how to approach support services.

Colleges have different ways to support you in the transition from high school. Recently, there has been a prolific increase in on-campus writing offerings, opportunities, and support services. Freshman composition courses, writing labs, and writing centers exist at many colleges. Martha, a college freshman, reflects, "Frankly, I was surprised that there were so many ways to get help with my writing, but I had to meet the people halfway who were trying to help me."

Freshman Composition

Many colleges offer writing courses for freshmen. Because professors still debate the best procedure for teaching writing, the formats of such courses vary both within and among colleges. Indeed, even the experts are unsure exactly where and by whom writing should be taught. Some believe that all college professors should teach writing; others contend that writing instruction is the responsibility of the English department. Still others approach the teaching of writing in an interdisciplinary fashion. Colgate University, for example, has an interdisciplinary writing program staffed by geology, anthropology, biology, and English professors. The writing director describes the Colgate program as "one of a kind and experimental" because it is not associated with any department. In spite of the debate about who should teach writing, students and professors agree that the one course that guarantees formal writing instruction is freshman composition.

Polly, a UCLA senior, recalls, "I got bits and pieces from other courses, but the only time I was actually taught writing in college was in my first-year comp course." At many institutions, students have just one semester during their freshman year to learn about writing. If and when a second writing course is offered, it usually is incorporated into the major during sophomore year. A required freshman literature course often complements the freshman composition course by teaching the rudiments of literary analysis with an emphasis on writing.

Although there is no standard curriculum for freshman composition, colleges are committed to introducing students to argumentation, structure, and other rudiments of writing. Reviewing the seven elements of good writing outlined in Chapter 2 is a first step in preparing for these courses. Forming the backbone of your college writing experience, freshman comp courses share a mission even if they don't share a syllabus: to build confidence; to foster self-discovery and self-knowledge; to identify, use, and apply the elements of effective writing.

After handing in your first composition assignment, take the time to ask for feedback. Don't allow your professors to keep information on your writing to themselves. Establishing a relationship with your professors from the start can keep you from feeling terror at your professor's door when you need assistance. Finding out your professor's views about your writing—both your strengths and weaknesses—will allow you to focus immediately and write in the light instead of the dark.

Let's look at a few composition assignments to understand further how you will learn about writing. Susan Beegel, a former composition instructor at Yale, describes her first freshman composition assignment as "diagnostic, motivating, and enlightening." She sends her students into the college community to interview working writers. The assignment helps students learn that all writers struggle with their craft. Students use basic writing skills and learn about the importance of asking provocative questions to elicit interesting answers. Students also discover how to narrow a subject area and locate a thesis while eliminating irrelevant information.

If you don't find yourself in a composition course like Ms. Beegel's, how might all of this apply to you? You can come to know yourself better as a writer by talking to others about writing (a theme stressed in Chapter 5). It may be reassuring to know that an accomplished writer is not necessarily a natural writer; even your professors labor over drafts and revisions. Even if you talk to only your own roommate about her writing, you have still benefited from Professor Beegel's assignment. You will learn the importance of asking questions. You will also develop important skills in logic and elaboration.

Assume, for example, that you are asked to write about arrogance. As you look at the first draft of your composition, ask yourself a series of questions: "Have I clearly defined and given concrete examples of arrogance?" "Have I substantiated my thesis that arrogance often gets in the way of positive character development?" Asking these questions might help you avoid a professor's commenting on your essay, "I don't really understand what you mean by the term *arrogance*. Could you develop this idea with an example? Where is the logic, the cause/effect relationship between being arrogant and not developing personally?"

At some colleges, your composition professor might emphasize structure and mechanics, focusing primarily on the formal product. Such courses teach thesis development, argumentation, substantiation, grammar, and essay format. Other freshman composition programs will teach the writing process—brainstorming, drafting, revising. These programs consider writer interaction to form the core of good writing skills. Journals, computers, and peer conferences will be at the heart of these courses. For the most part, your and your classmates' writing will constitute the course content. In courses such as these, "Writing will no longer be taught virtually as a correspondence course via marginal comments on your papers," explains Kathleen Skubikowski, director of writing at Middlebury College. In other words, you will become involved not only in your own writing but also in that of your classmates. These programs will vary between colleges and universities and also within the same institution. You must be ready for a variety of experiences.

Increasingly, professors are using freshman comp courses to teach students to select writing topics out of their own experiences. Journals, freewrites, and rough drafts become the course's text. You will write and share journal entries to promote interaction among you and your classmates. You will be asked to create both essays and fiction from these entries. In this way, you will learn to generate ideas and writing topics on your own and wean yourself from your teacher as a source for ideas, an important step to becoming a successful lifelong writer.

Open-ended assignments encourage creativity and original thinking. One approach is for your professor (or even other students) to offer several paragraphs of a story and then ask the class to finish it. Rather than worrying about what the professor wants, you immediately become involved in the details and excitement of solving the problem. In a political science or history assignment, you might be asked to role-play. What would you do if faced with Joan of Arc's choice? Or, if you were Napoleon, what would your next strategy be?

In other composition assignments, professors might ask you to analyze a philosopher's theory or a literary passage. Or, they might ask you to explain how Shakespeare uses language and imagery to develop mood in a particular play or scene. In that case, the professor would be looking for a specific type of response, a thesis supported by specifics from the text. The style and content of such an essay would be limited. However, you would select the passages to examine and the imagery to pursue.

Because it is impossible to tell what sort of freshman composition course you will take at the outset, you might want to attend a freshman writing course when you visit colleges or write the college you ultimately choose and ask about the requirements and formats of writing courses.

The burden placed on freshman writing courses to teach all the elements of effective writing has induced universities to form writing centers and labs and to train students as peer tutors and editors. Together, these groups share the teaching and increase the opportunity for students to improve their writing.

Writing Centers and Labs

Writing centers and labs are popping up on college campuses across the country. These centers and labs can vary from a small room with study carrels, tucked away in the library, to a brand new suite housing tutoring conference alcoves, a peer-tutor training classroom, offices, computers, and a writing library.

Such centers support both students and faculty and are directed by trained professionals. At some universities, they form the hub of the freshman writing program, offering students semester-long comp classes. For the most part, the course work trains students in the seven elements of effective writing outlined in Chapter 2. The method of instruction will vary, but the objectives remain consistent from one campus to another.

Writing Center: What Is It?

If you expect a writing center or lab to resemble a TV newspaper editing room, with keyboards clicking and tutors bustling from computer to computer, you will be surprised by the calm and quiet that surrounds these areas. This atmosphere seems to arise from the philosophy that drives most centers, "Writing is a long process, not a single act."

At the writing lab, you will find students engaged in many stages of the writing process. Some will be working with a tutor to brainstorm on a topic or discover a thesis; others, to develop and express their ideas; and others, to locate and integrate supporting evidence. Students will be in various stages of drafts or revision—focusing on organization, sentence clarity, and grammar. Some students will be working in an open lab setting while others will be conferring in a private alcove or reading their essay aloud to a tutor at one of the writing stations. Martha, a peer tutor, explains, "We almost always ask students to read their papers out loud because it is the best way to locate trouble areas. We know that professors hate to struggle with the reading."

Writing centers are dedicated to teaching students

the relationship between writing and thinking, how to write clearly and concisely, and how to speak specifically about their writing. To these ends, writing centers offer opportunities for students at all writing levels. From a drop-in appointment to discuss a dull paper to a weekly tutorial taken for credit in conjunction with a writing seminar, the center is as viable for seniors as for freshmen. It can be a place to address and polish troublesome grammatical errors or to develop writing skills that match the increased complexity of course material and your own advanced thinking. One junior at a small midwestern college recalls, "The writing center helped me develop the writing skills and style I needed to meet my 20-year-old ideas, which I had been trying to express with the skills and style of a 16-year-old. It was hard for me to admit this and to overcome the stigma of going for 'extra help,' but once I did, I became a regular."

For many students the biggest stumbling block in college is to admit needing help and then seeking assistance. A high school senior from Rhode Island confesses, "Seeking writing help is hard for me. I have no problem asking for help with math or French. It isn't the remedial nature of the writing center that's hanging me up, it's the personal nature of writing. When I think of getting help with my writing, it's as if I'm revealing a very private part of myself. Sometimes I'm amazed that I let my teachers even read my papers." Keep in mind that the professionals and peer tutors who staff writing centers are trained to help you with your writing without destroying your own work.

Writing Center: Getting There

If you end up in a writing-intensive course, the problem of reaching out for writing help might be solved for you: you may not need to find the support, it may find you. Many colleges and universities assign teaching assistants to students to help them with their writing assignments. The operative theory is that these tutors will know both content and writing; will be familiar with the class and the context of the assignments; and will be able to explain "what the professor wants."

When the writing program and freshman composition are both housed in the writing center, a natural bond occurs between writing, the student, and the center. Students also have the advantage of meeting professors and tutors in a writing-oriented setting.

It might be more difficult to find your way to the writing lab if it's a small room in the library. Apprehension and/or embarrassment could keep you from making contact. However, a professor may refer you to the lab, suggesting that you go there to develop a thesis, sharpen diction, tighten logic, or strengthen a writing voice. This can help you establish a relationship with the writing center. In some courses, professors allow you to rewrite a paper if your grade is lower than B. In both of these situations, a professional or peer writing tutor can make all the difference.

Sometimes it takes a disaster to lead you to the writing lab or center. A frantic senior who dropped in when his thesis proposal had been rejected talks about having lost his confidence. He was both defensive and confused. "I've gotten A's and B's in all my political science courses since freshman year and now that I'm a senior, they're telling me I can't write." Although this might seem like an extreme case, you might find yourself in a similar situation. Mike, a Middlebury College freshman, said that he sought out the writing center because he had always gotten honor grades in high school, and now he was getting C's on essays and lab reports. Mike's student adviser introduced him to a friend who was a peer tutor. After the tutor made a "house call," Mike went to the lab for help.

Writing labs maintain regular hours. Once you locate the center, ask about the hours and the drop-in and appointment policies, and then start using the center as you need it. Remember, becoming a better writer is ultimately your responsibility. You might want to get a preliminary assessment of your first paper, or perhaps you simply can't get started on a writing assignment, or a paper just isn't flowing. These and many others are valid reasons for visiting your writing center.

Peer Tutors

Colleges are also connecting peer tutors with writing-intensive courses. One tutor describes her experience with a freshman political science course. She attended all the classes and then had biweekly office hours to help students with their writing. Each week students wrote a short essay, a "concise rendering of the material in question." She worked with students to help them understand what the professor wanted, and offered general writing advice and reactions to students' essays. In class, the students read their papers aloud as part of the discussion. From the start, the course became a writing community. By mid-semester, the tutor was "amazed how both the writing and the quality of discussion had improved and how good thinking and good writing had become synonymous." Students learned the advantage of having peer evaluators. Becoming a better writer became a primary objective.

Writing centers and labs often offer handouts on common writing assignments and problems, sample questions and responses, sample lab reports, and stylesheets. Using this information, a tutor might help you develop a process for answering essay-test questions or for reading and interpreting assignments. In many institutions, the writing center becomes a library of writing resources. Everything from dictionaries to style manuals to word-processing and writing software to reference books are there for your use. Peer tutors are trained to help students use these materials.

Sensitive and experienced writers themselves, peer tutors are committed to helping students become good writers. One senior tutor explains, "Tutoring is a way for me to stay on top of my writing. When I help others with their writing, I learn more about my own writing. I often bring my own papers to the lab to go over with one of the peer tutors." Dora, another tutor, agrees: "I find that by helping others I help myself. I have learned how to ask myself questions about my writing. I work with other tutors to understand my own writing process and style and then use this knowledge to help others."

Training sessions for peer tutors emphasize listening, asking questions, and coping with writer stress. "Often, students come to the writing lab expecting me to write or rewrite the paper for them," reports Jennifer, a tutor at a Southwestern university. The first rule for all tutors is: never pick up a pencil. The second rule is: never tell a student what to write.

When you work with a tutor, you can expect the tutor to ask you to:

- Describe the assignment or explain it in detail.
- Show what you have done up to this point.
- Read your essay out loud.
- Identify and discuss your thesis.
- Talk about your frustration/writer's block/idea block.
- Talk out your ideas; say what you want the writing to say and mean.

As you proceed with a tutoring session or develop a relationship with a tutor, the writing topics you cover will be vast. If you are in search of a topic for an essay, you might be asked to freewrite for several minutes. Then, the tutor might help you go over the freewrite to find your central ideas. You might then be asked to freewrite again—this time on one of the main ideas—so that you can begin to make even more decisions about which ideas are weak and which are strong. By doing so, a tutor can help you develop a writing process.

A tutor might suggest ways to reorganize or present your essay. You might discuss logic and audience. The tutor's perspective can help you better understand audience. The tutor might point out unclear terminology, jargon, or confusing diction. As one tutor explains, "When a student comes with a paper that is unclear or stilted, I ask him to tell me what he means. As soon as he does, I tell him to write down exactly what he said. Most students are amazed by the difference this makes."

How much help can you expect from a tutor? Very simply, a tutor will do just about anything except write your paper. The writing center or lab staff, both professional and peer, can teach you how to improve your writing. A clear, logical product is only one of the outcomes.

Remember, a tutor will not take responsibility for any low grade you might receive. The tutor is there to function as a sounding board, to react to the clarity and logic of the writing, to probe and question. He or she is not there to do the thinking or writing for you.

You can count on a great deal of writing support when you get to college, but, ultimately, you are the one who must reach out. Freshman comp, writing centers, and peer tutors are there to help, but you must make the most of them. Only one person can make you a better writer: you.

Word
Processing

A small screen, a blinking cursor, a three-inch square plastic disk, and a keyboard have revolutionized writing. "Over 90 percent of our students now word process," reports Tom Blackburn, professor of English at Swarthmore College. Why are so many students using computers? Why is it worth investing time and even money to learn how to word process? Theo, a college junior from the Midwest, explains, "When I was faced with a blank piece of paper, I used to freeze. Now, when I face an empty screen, the flashing cursor keeps saying, 'Write, write, write. You can do it, you can do it,' and I've discovered I can."

Many professors like word processing because it encourages revision, the cornerstone of good writing. When you don't have to retype a whole essay in order to make changes, the entire writing process is more inviting, not to mention less time-consuming. For these very practical reasons, professors and students recommend that you come to college knowing something about word processing or at least with a willingness to learn word-processing skills early in your freshman year.

This chapter covers the significant reasons for including word processing in your writing, outlines the controversy surrounding word processing, and discusses how you might become a better writer by merging the art of writing with technology. Word processing can help your writing, but you have to decide for yourself if it works for you.

"Working Knowledge" Defined

Professors recommend that you come to college with a "working knowledge" of word processing. In other words, they expect that you know the keyboard; that you can load a word-processing program; that you understand and can use basic commands (e.g., delete, replace, page up, page down, scroll, move); that you can control cursor movement; and that you have a sense of the special features that a word-processing program offers, even if you are not proficient in using them (e.g., footnotes, dictionary, spell-check, margins, tabs). Judy Sinnock, a word-processing instructor at a Vermont high school, comments, "Speed is not the issue; time and practice will take care of that. What is important is for you to know the keyboard and be able to use it without looking at your hands. Hunting for keys interrupts and can even disrupt the creative process." With this basic knowledge, word processing can make a difference in your writing.

The Case against Word Processing

For some writers, the computer invades their privacy, is an inconvenience, or insults their integrity. Good writing, as you know, means making choices. Choosing whether or not to use word processing is a choice every writer must make. Take time to develop a writing process, as explained in Chapter 3, so that you can choose the writing tools and develop the writing skills that are best for you. What follows are two of the most often stated reasons students and professors give for *not* using word processing.

- **Intrusion.** "The flashing cursor drives me crazy." "It constantly nags at me to write." "You can no longer choose the location of your writing; you are chained to the machine—whether it be in a computer lab, your room, the library, a classroom." "I hate green lettering." "There is no way to doodle in the margins."

"When I use a computer with a mouse, it reduces writing to a video game. How trendy can you get?" These are some of the negative comments about word processing offered by students. For many of these students (and even professors), using a pen or pencil is natural and calming. As a senior history major explains, "When I write with a pen or pencil, my writing slows down so that I am careful and involved in what I say."

- **False security.** "In most test and exam situations, you cannot use word processing. You rely on your own organizational skills, not technology," advises an economics major. Depending on technology for good writing seems inhibiting or even crippling for some students.

    "It makes papers 'look good' without much effort," warn several professors. Beware of typing directly into the computer and then pushing the print button. This should come as no surprise to you after reading the definition of effective writing outlined in Chapter 2. It is easy, however, to confuse polished print with polished text. If you have labored over typewritten papers, with the smudges of corrasible paper and white-out, you understand how this could happen.

Are you old-fashioned or conservative if you are anti–word processing? No. Part of your personal writing process may involve putting pen to paper. As you take charge of your writing, you will have to make decisions. You may decide to use word processing, as many students do, in the final revision stages to avoid the cost and time of typing and retyping. Or, you may begin to use it merely for minor revisions—to correct typos and careless spelling and grammar mistakes. You can include word processing in your writing process to varying degrees.

How Word Processing Can Help

"Perhaps the most crucial thing for freshmen to be aware of is how important writing will be to them, not only in college courses but in any profession they are likely to choose," suggests Catherine Campbell of Middlebury's Chinese department. As most students and professors agree, word processing helps people become better writers, and it stands to reason that you should try any tool that might improve your writing. Again, you need to decide what writing tools work best for you, but consider the following experiences while making your decision.

Spontaneity

"When using the word processor my writing seems to jump from my head to the screen." "I am able to write my thoughts as I think them." "I get ideas down faster and they seem more natural." "Watching the words appear before me somehow makes my thinking and writing one. I don't feel so tongue-tied." For these students who advocate word processing, spontaneity leads to greater confidence in their writing.

Freewriting

When you freewrite, you want to write as much as you can as quickly as you can. (See Chapter 3 for a complete discussion of freewriting.) You want to let your mind go and write whatever comes into your head. In a focused freewrite, you write on only one topic, idea, or question. Regardless of what kind of freewriting you are doing, word processing can help. If you type 30 words per minute, you are probably typing faster than you can write by hand.

This can keep you from losing important ideas because your hand becomes tired or because your writing can't keep up with your thinking. When you are finished, you have a clean, legible copy. Now, you can move ideas around, elaborate on them, and/or delete them. "Word processing makes me a more efficient writer. I can take words and phrases—sometimes even whole sentences—from my freewrites, categorize them, and form rough paragraphs," explains Eric, a University of Texas sophomore. For some students, rough outlines emerge from these freewrites. When you don't have to copy and rewrite, organization is easier.

Collaboration

"My freshman composition course centered around word processing and what my professor called 'interactive writing.' We met in a computer lab, wrote to each other via a computer hookup, and constantly tried to improve our writing by working with one another. Even the professor joined the network." For Tom, this interaction formed the backbone of his college writing. "Word processing became the center of my writing process. With so much of the tedium removed from the process, I was able to focus on the words and my style."

Tom's experience reemphasizes a major theme of *The Student's Guide to Good Writing*: good writers share their writing and seek criticism from other writers. It also illustrates the frequency with which professors are using the computer to teach writing. Allison, a University of Vermont sophomore, relates how her writing tutor sits at the computer and conducts an initial revision. "I usually read the piece aloud while my tutor listens, makes notes, and then asks questions about the logic and clarity of the writing. Somehow I find this less threatening."

Word processing also facilitates group writing. At

many colleges, group projects are common. Students work together hovered around one screen or share disks (and hard copies) to compile a collective report. At Rensselaer Polytechnic Institute, students take freshman seminars that culminate in group papers. Each student answers one question out of four on a similar topic. Each question becomes a short paper and receives an individual grade, but the examination demands that the group shares information. This encourages students to take responsibility for good writing—and for each other. Word processing can help in several phases of group projects: brainstorming and organizing; sharing ideas and revising; and exchanging drafts and final copies.

"In my freshman composition course, we were asked to take a classmate's disk, access a file, and insert comments about the writing," explains Manuel, a Rollins College junior. In this way, Manuel's professor encourages interaction, sharpens critical skills, and gives students specific revision help. In addition, the professor writes a comment to each of her students. The best way to improve your own writing is by helping friends with theirs.

Multiple Papers

In all likelihood, you will have to keep several writing assignments going simultaneously. You may find yourself in the middle of one paper while spawning ideas for another. Word processing offers an organizational solution to this dilemma. "I used to jot down ideas on scraps of paper and put them in my desk drawer. Finally, I got organized and kept the ideas on different pads of paper. Then, I misplaced the pads and had to start all over again. Now, I create a new file and just type in ideas as I get them," explains Adam, a word-processing convert from New

Hampshire. A printout of such random thoughts provides an excellent departure point for an essay or report. You can look for common ideas, relationships, and even contradictions that offer focus for freewrites or thesis statements.

If you write from an outline, you can enter an essay or report outline into the computer. As you research your topic, you can add ideas, quotations, and specific details under appropriate headings. When you begin to write, rough paragraphs will be in front of you. Jennifer, a chemistry major, enters her lab report outline and then adds data as she proceeds with her experiment. She advocates this approach: "I have much of the report written by the time the experiment has been completed." Now, Jennifer just has to add conclusions, revise, and print.

Revision

Although most writers find revision tedious and frustrating, word processing can eliminate some of the agony. Three word-processing supporters explain. "The computer gives me more chances to revise either on the screen or on a hard copy." "Word processing makes every step in my writing process more efficient." "I'm not afraid to proofread because I can make corrections easily and quickly."

Who wants to struggle with your handwriting, crossouts, and insertions if they can review a neatly printed copy instead? Dannelle, a college junior, confesses, "My handwriting is illegible chicken scratch. My roommate refuses to read my papers unless I have a clean copy. I don't blame her, because I don't have that kind of time either. Word processing has been my salvation." Wide margins and triple spacing allow room for your reader's comments and your own revisions, before you go back to the computer. You will find it easier to work from a printed copy than from a heavily edited manuscript.

The Big Seven

When you begin revising for the Big Seven, there are ways the computer and word processing can help.

- **Logic.** One of the hardest things to do when you are writing is to maintain your focus. When writing an essay by hand, you have to keep shuffling pages to look back at your thesis statement. Several word-processing programs can help you with this problem. For example, if you use Microsoft Word, a Mac/IBM compatible software program, you can split the screen so that your thesis literally remains in front of you. "This keeps me from wandering and saves me a lot of revising," explains Jeff, a sophomore from a midwestern college.

   A student from the University of Massachusetts explains how she combines the split-screen feature with the topic sentence outline strategy discussed in Chapter 3. "I put my topic sentences in boldface as a way of reminding myself of my focus. With the thesis in front of me, I can quickly check whether my topic sentences relate to it. Finding my topic sentences quickly helps me test my writing for focus and logic."

- **Diction.** A word-processing program's dictionary and thesaurus options can help you improve your diction, or word awareness. Like the spelling and grammar check, these programs offer options for different words. Neither the dictionary and thesaurus nor the spelling and grammar check make corrections. You, the writer, must interact and make choices; this, in turn, can help you learn vocabulary and improve your writing. "For me, the dictionary and thesaurus features make word choice manageable and challenging. Ordinarily, I am too impatient to stop and search for new words," confesses a University of Michigan freshman.

- **Boldness.** Boldness requires experimentation. As a student from Virginia explains, "When using a computer, I can easily pound out an idea and print it. If my ideas or style are outrageous, I can easily modify or delete the piece. After I write out something in longhand, I hate to throw it away."

- **Elaboration.** Professors often ask for additional examples, anecdotes, or quotations. Word processing can help you meet their demand for greater depth. Using the insert mode, you can add information and print a new copy. This is particulary helpful when your examples are too general and your ideas are underdeveloped. A student from Connecticut explains, "For elaboration, I scroll down and leave space to add more details and layers of argumentation or support. This forces me to discuss more."

- **Mechanics.** Spell checks and grammar checks can speed up mechanical revisions. When you use these programs, the computer highlights a potential trouble spot. You are then given choices from which to select a correct form. In this way, you are involved in the correction process and you can improve your spelling and grammar awareness. "I know my spelling is terrible and professors show no mercy in their comments and grading. The spell check saves me from embarrassment and low grades," remarks Heyward, a student from Florida.

Hard and Fast Rules of Word Processing

Like the person operating the computer, word processing is fallible. You need to take necessary precautions to avoid running into mechanical difficulties.

- **Keep back-up disks.** Disks are fragile and easily lost. Computers and programs can "crash" as you write. A destroyed disk is a poor excuse for a late writing assignment. Protect your writing and yourself: *always* keep a current and updated back-up disk.

- **Save.** Take appropriate steps to "save" your writing according to the particular program you are using. If you don't, you could lose all you have written in a momentary power failure or by accidentally pushing a wrong key. Students who word process tell horror stories about a computer going "down" and taking their 10-page paper with it. Every time you pause to think, enter the appropriate command to "save" the writing you have entered.

- **Print a hard copy.** Hard copy is a printout of what you have written. Make a printed copy of everything you write, so that if a disk is lost or damaged, you aren't left empty-handed. Also, after you have made changes in a revision step, print a copy to test the effectiveness of these changes. Make notes in the margin or mark unclear or awkward places so that when you revise, you keep your revision focused. The checklist at the end of Chapter 3 can help you with this.

Conclusion

Computers can be found in classrooms, writing labs, libraries, and even the dormitories of most college campuses. You do not need to purchase your own hardware. Many colleges are helping students buy computers at special prices with interest-free loans. This enables you to make a lifelong investment in writing and in a technological skill.

Professors and students agree that you will achieve clarity and precision in your writing over time and through multiple revisions. Rereading what you have written (and having others do the same) helps you locate what one student calls "mine fields" in your writing. Word processing can facilitate rereading by providing clean printed copy, and it can eliminate such deterrents to revision as "copying over" and "retyping," because making changes is so easy.

A word to those of you who decide not to word process. Give word processing an occasional try—you might change your mind. One professor tells how it took him until graduate school to feel "confident and competent sitting at a computer. Now I can't imagine writing without one."

If you suffer from computer phobia, consider watching a friend word process, taking a course in word processing, and/or working with a tutor in your writing center.

And, finally, a word of caution: word processing is not magic. Be sure that the computer does not become the writer. Maintain control so that your own thoughts, not the disk drive, are the force driving your writing. Only you—not the computer—can transform a rough draft into a final polished piece.

Going Beyond Good Writing

College students say that junior and senior writing differs from freshman and sophomore writing in personal style, individual voice, and confidence—writing abilities that professors look for. These writing qualities come with maturity and from practice. There is no easy formula for making the transition from college writing to lifelong good writing. You can, however, learn how to progress from the experiences of juniors and seniors.

Before exploring specific techniques that facilitate the transition, you might want to hear a few perspectives on this evolution from several advanced writers, mostly juniors and seniors who were immersed in thesis writing and seminar papers. One student, a senior history major, said: "You reach a point where writing's no longer a chore; it's therapy. I truly enjoy it—I'm hooked."

Sarah, a junior in the beginning stages of her thesis, tells about her writing experiences: "As a beginning college writer, I wrote many small papers. I dashed them off before class, late at night, early in the morning. I rarely revised or rewrote my essays; I rarely felt the pressure to do so. Now I'm on the fifth revision of my thesis prospectus and it's only five pages! My thesis advisers are looking not only for content, focus, and conciseness, but also for an individual voice and style. They are pushing me to make this *my* piece of writing."

Many beginning students discover that developing their own writing voice and style is an intimidating prospect. "I can no longer claim that I don't know what professors want," explains one college student. "I know—they want a voice and a style that is mine alone." However, students in their final college years realize that they can no longer be told how to write; it must come from within.

Jim, a senior from Massachusetts, accepts this challenge confidently. "When I got to college, I had a 'writer's ear.' I could always tell if something sounded right. What I couldn't do was explain why it was so. Now, I have a

123

'writer's eye.' I can see things around me, and I can write about them. I can understand why writing sounds good or correct. I can talk about my writing and the writing of others."

Going beyond good writing means identifying oneself as a writer and facing a 10-page paper with the same confidence with which you once faced a 2-page paper. It means intuitively applying all the elements of effective writing to this longer assignment. Writing becomes an art form. One senior claims, "By letting go of an inhibiting structure, like the five-paragraph essay, the paper almost writes itself." Another student remarks, "You follow a different format for each paper and that's okay. In fact, the variety sustains the writing. When I was a freshman I was convinced that every paper was set up and written following the same format."

Risk Taking

If you accept that each paper will be different, you can spend your time experimenting and exploring new forms and new ideas. Students believe that the key to doing this is content. Increased knowledge allows you to write more integrated essays and formulate sophisticated thesis statements. This, in turn, can lead you to experiment with new forms.

A sociology professor groans, "I am so tired of reading clear, coherent, and grammatically correct papers that are dull!" Some students leave high school so competent in form and grammar that they write on automatic pilot. Dullness comes from the inability to establish a voice and a level of creativity that does justice to your knowledge. It comes from the inability or unwillingness to risk a strong personal position on the paper topic or in the writing style.

Professors have different approaches to helping student writers develop complex thesis statements that lead to more lively writing voices and styles. One method is to freewrite on your topic from one point of view. Write as much as you can in 15 minutes without lifting your pen from the paper or your fingers from the keyboard. When you are freewriting, you don't have to worry about grammar or spelling or how you've worded an idea; all you do is focus on ideas and content. As Debra M. Bailin, director of the writing center at Vermont's Lyndon State College notes, when you freewrite, "You are just stretching." Stretching yourself is an important step to risk taking. After freewriting on your topic from one point of view, freewrite on the topic for another 15 minutes from the *opposite* point of view. Experimenting with different points of view is essential in producing mature writing. Experimentation will help lead you to a more interesting thesis.

For example, in a sociology course, a writer might freewrite to explore the topic of abortion. If he were a strong pro-choice advocate, his writing would touch on the many reasons why elective abortion is a woman's right. He would probably address rape, incest, teenage pregnancy, birth defects, and the mother's health and well-being. Now, however, the freewrite should shift to the other point of view, pro-life. This freewrite would explore the right to life, the point at which life begins, the rights of the fetus, adoption, and the rights of the father. From these two freewrites, the writer could now develop a thesis that encompasses both sides of the argument. The writer might then discover an innovative way to begin the paper. He might open with a creative depiction of a woman dealing with an unwanted pregnancy, confronting the pro-life and pro-choice demonstrators outside the clinic. This approach would eliminate the complaint of dullness that can plague sociology writing. The decision the woman makes and the reasons she makes it would define the thesis.

You might say this is fine for the person who can rationally take both sides of an argument, but what if the topic is so controversial, so emotional—as in the case of the abortion issue—that objectivity is impossible? If so, you might want to ask another person to freewrite an opposing point of view for you. Not only will this encourage you to approach the essay anticipating the argument against your position, but it will also open the door for dialogue and/or debate. Having engaged in this process, you will find it easier to write an essay that is driven by a confident, personal voice or an individual style.

The major requirement in risk taking involves a willingness to stretch yourself to include a different point of view, and to present your ideas in a novel way by discarding the safety of a clear, concise, but conventional presentation that your audience has already heard.

Style

The degree to which you are able to develop a personal style depends, in part, on the academic discipline for which you write. To a biology major, advanced writing means longer lab reports, with fairly rigid formats. Even if you publish in scientific journals, the demand for specific and concise information controls the writing. Economics and business writing demand the same precision as the natural sciences. In these disciplines, you are presenting research, explaining formulas, and reviewing literature; the writing model is predetermined. Dana, a junior economics major, explains, "Content controls my writing; I have to think in economic terms about what is going on, and express the facts in the simplest, most direct way possible." Mark, a junior business major, agrees, "In business, you don't want your audience to notice you, the writer. Your information, written clearly and succinctly, carries the writing. Style is a factor but a secondary factor." If you are writing for a literature, political science, or history course, you may have more opportunities to experiment with style.

When you begin developing a personal style, you are making a conscious decision to write to be noticed. Writing becomes easier because you are no longer writing just for the assignment or the grade. You know where you want to go with the writing; hence, you are freer to think about how you are saying it. Instead of writing, "Recycling reduces solid waste and protects natural resources," you might want to create a visual image for your reader: "Picture piles of newspapers littered around a park devoid of trees."

You need to be comfortable with your subject matter in order to take your writing beyond mere technical accuracy. Finding this comfort level occurs over time, which is why advanced writing accompanies advanced thinking and generally occurs in the junior and senior years. One college senior offers this explanation: "In my first year of college, I wrote a lot of small papers in order to learn how to structure and organize my writing. We were given a short poem, a political speech, or an economics article and directed to pay close attention to specific words and passages. Rarely did we create our own focus or topic. Now as a senior I'm more at liberty to determine and control the content of my writing. My style is determined by the journals, newspapers, and secondary sources I decide to consult; how I choose to organize and integrate the material; and how I narrow the topic but also present the broader picture."

There are several ways to liberate your writing style:

- **Begin with a brief abstraction.** Some students employ methods used in creative writing courses. "Although I have to be careful not to distort the facts in my

127

history papers, I can include colorful language to catch my reader's attention. By interrupting the analysis with a description of a court trial, I engage my reader," said Sarah, a junior history major at Swarthmore. "I find myself constantly trying to hold the reader's attention." An example of this approach would be to describe a moment in the Salem witch trials. "The citizenry flocked to the courthouse in the chill of January to witness the trial of Rebecca Nurse. Fear hovered over them as they walked with heads down and collars up. No one took time to greet friends and neighbors. Clearly, this was not an arraignment of witchcraft but of the Salemites' own hypocrisy."

- **Try a new format.** As your particular style emerges, the only way to advance your writing is to experiment. Kea, a political science major explains, "My professors encourage risk taking. They tell us, 'We give B's to technically correct papers and A's to papers that are interesting to read.' By trying different styles and formats, I come closer to defining my own style." You might try a dialogue, a debate, a letter to the editor, or a manifesto. Instead of listing facts in a paper on the Chicago Seven, you might set it up as a conversation between Abbie Hoffman and Mayor Daly.

- **Deviate from conventional writing rules.** Beckett, a political science major, has made the three-sentence paragraph part of her style. Most often, she uses it to emphasize a point. "Two years ago I would have been afraid to do this," she says. "Now, however, I am in control. I know why I am doing it and when it is appropriate. It's not something I could have done as a freshman."

- **Take risks in the introduction and conclusion.** Don't be afraid to start with a bold first sentence or to make a new observation in the conclusion. "I no longer just review and summarize in my conclusion," writes a philosophy major, "I use the conclusion to provoke my reader, to inspire a response." Instead of ending your philosophy paper with, "Plato is a great philosopher because he still inspires us to think," try "How often have you walked through the cave?"

- **Develop a writing format and style to complement the content.** For example, when asked to analyze a play, you might create a dialogue between two of the play's characters or even go a step further and invent a new scene that presents a critical element. Following a more traditional avenue, you might adopt the voice of a drama critic and present your analysis in the form of a review.

Voice

"In high school and even through my freshman year at college, all of my teachers urged me to avoid using the personal pronoun *I* in my essays, except for special instances. The first person, however, gives me my personal writing voice," explains a religion major. *I* can serve as a tool for your emerging voice; like any tool, it has limitations, but it can be effective if used at the right time. Some professors contend that the personal pronoun conveys maturity, experience, and even self-knowledge.

As you develop a personal style, you will find your writing voice. "I'm not sure if I found a writing voice through experimentation with style or if by finding my writing voice, I was able to create my own style," explains Suzanne, a senior majoring in creative writing.

In upper-level courses, good writers gradually let go

129

of conventional style and their stilted academic voice. Assignments become open-ended; professors do not assign specific topics for essays or creative pieces. Instead, you formulate and select a topic based on the reading or discussion, thus taking charge of your writing. As writing assignments change, you change as a writer. When you write for a purpose other than a grade, you take an important step in establishing a lifelong writing voice.

In an essay on Chaucer, for example, you could incorporate your own philosophy. The "Wife of Bath" becomes a starting point for presenting your own feminist manifesto. Take a stand and a voice begins to emerge. Present ideas and facts from your course work, discussions, reading, and interactions to defend your position. When you do this, a lifelong writing voice begins to evolve.

Below are five specific steps to help develop your writing voice:

1. **Write in your journal daily.** Routinely expressing personal feelings allows you to gain confidence in your opinions. This, in turn, will develop into a more confident writing voice. "The more I write for myself and not for professors, the more I take charge of my writing, and the more clearly I write," explains Fred, an art history major at Columbia University.

2. **Try new voices when writing essays.** Experiment with humor, sarcasm. "As long as the content is correct, I find that professors accept different voices," writes Mark, a political science major. "What I can no longer tolerate in my writing is the mimicked textbook voice."

3. **Carefully choose the facts you use.** An art history major says, "For the longest time, I felt controlled by the enormous number of historical facts. I didn't think that I could do anything but present the facts and my hypothesis. Now, as a senior, I realize that

the facts I choose establish my writing voice." Your writing voice will evolve as you integrate these facts into your essay.

4. **Forget about audience for the first few drafts.** "I write with more confidence and with a stronger voice when I write for myself rather than some invisible audience. If I have to, in the final draft, I adjust my writing to fit an audience. I find more and more that such adjustments are not necessary."

5. **Write as often as possible.** The more you write, the better you write. "Because I am finally comfortable with writing, as comfortable as I am throwing a ball, I have a natural voice that I am not afraid to use," comments a sociology major who also pitches for the varsity baseball team.

Confidence

"I now think of myself as a writer more than I think about my writing," quips a junior English major. Confidence marks the transition from humdrum to pizzaz, from tenderfoot to lifelong writer.

Create your own pieces from your head and heart. The degree to which you take risks in writing, just as in life, depends on self-confidence. Where does this writing confidence come from? How does one build confidence in writing? How does one overcome the fear of writing?

As you have read repeatedly in *The Student's Guide to Good Writing*, time is a crucial variable in the confidence equation. There is no guarantee that you will graduate from college with good lifelong writing skills. Your academic path may not give you the exposure that naturally produces the gains you are seeking and, even if you have been exposed to writing by taking an appropriate sequence of courses, you may avoid taking the writer's leap of faith.

Aside from attitude and maturity, these factors usually affect writing confidence:

- **Specialization.** Soon after your freshman year, you will be asked to select a major, minor, and/or concentration. As you take more courses in one academic area, you will gain more confidence about what you know. Because of your accumulated knowledge, you will be convinced that you have something to write about. As you begin to specialize and pursue your personal interests, you will develop relationships with friends and professors who share these interests—whether they be in economics, Eastern religions, Chinese, computers, or women's literature. This will bolster your confidence, for you will begin to look upon yourself as an adult learner. You may also seek to distinguish yourself from your circle of friends and thus be prompted to take more risks in your writing. In short, you will create your own writing signature.

- **Equal status.** Again, as you move from freshman to senior year, the barriers between you and your professors will break down. Expanded knowledge and developing experience will give you the confidence to sit down with a professor as an equal and talk about your writing. You can go beyond a discussion of technical methods and talk about style, voice, and risk taking. This relationship is a two-way street. One writing professor talks about joining the writing community of his class and sharing a finished manuscript, only to elicit "valid recommendations from his students for revision."

- **Creative writing.** Like other art forms, creative writing promotes intimacy, dialogue, and communication. You will become part of a community of writers from whom you will gain confidence in yourself as a writer. You will realize that your purpose is to experiment with style and voice, to take risks. This, in itself, will build confidence. Taking courses in creative writing can also help you become a lifelong writer.

Conclusion

The challenge of becoming a successful lifelong writer can inspire you to pursue your writing beyond academic confines. Being aware of the possibilities and potential for growth as a writer and writing for more than grades and professors could lead you on an exciting journey.

Student
to
Student

There is no doubt that it takes time, effort, and patience to become a successful lifelong writer.

Many good writing skills and habits develop as the result of increased writing experience. In other words: the more you write, the better you write. However, you may be wondering what you can do in the meantime. You may still feel uneasy about what professors will expect when you arrive on campus.

This chapter will alleviate some of your anxiety by offering responses of college writers to the 10 questions most often asked by high school juniors and seniors. Their answers to the questions posed below will provide you with specific strategies, skills, and information, as you map your personal writing strategy for college.

Question #1: "I don't have to write very much at my high school. What can I do to get ready for college writing?"

Gigi, a high school senior from rural Georgia, had not written a paper since her freshman English class. "I was sure that I was limited not only in my college choices but in my chances for success. Fortunately, my guidance counselor told me about the Governor's Institute, held every summer in Atlanta. After six weeks of writing at the institute, I feel so much better about my writing and my chances for success at college."

Many states sponsor summer institutes. Write your state department of education to inquire about writing programs sponsored by your state or by nearby colleges and universities. As noted in Chapter 6, there are numerous summer programs available, and the list grows yearly.

If you do not want to give up your summer, ask your high school teachers for help. Because they know you, they will be able to direct you to appropriate books or give you practical advice. Some may even have time to work with you during a free period or after school, once they know that you are interested and have the motivation to improve your writing. "My English teacher lent me one of his college writing books. He suggested chapters and exercises that were helpful," explains a college freshman. "Knowing I was making an effort to prepare myself for what was ahead relieved some of my anxiety."

"The director of our high school computer center showed me a writing-process software program. During my free periods, I worked with this program. By the time I got to college, I knew the different writing steps—brainstorming, drafting, revising—even though I needed to practice them. Any student who goes to a school that doesn't teach a lot of writing should find a way to learn the writing process before getting to college," advises a college sophomore.

Question #2: "I've only written short papers in high school. How will I ever be able to write a 5-page essay let alone a 20-page term paper? How much will I write in college and how long will writing assignments be?"

A college sophomore from Oregon recalls, "In most freshman courses we only wrote 2- or 3-page papers. This helped develop my writing skills and confidence. When I began writing 10- and 15-page papers, I thought of them in terms of five 2-page papers or five 3-page papers. This made the whole task more manageable."

"By the end of sophomore year," explains Tanya, a UCLA student, "I knew I wanted to major in Asian studies. I started to develop a pool of knowledge and found that length was not the issue. The challenge was trying to write clearly and boldly."

Khalid, a college junior, describes his early fears about the quantity of writing expected in college and offers simple advice: "Keep a journal. I arrived on campus sure that I would never be able to write an 8-page paper. When I completed a 60-page journal in my freshman composition course, I realized that I had something to say, even if I had to learn more about how to say it."

College professors indicate there is no standard amount of time spent on writing, and there is no fixed assignment length. Most college students spend 40 to 50 percent of their academic time writing; the one exception is for English majors, for whom the percentage is 60. There is also considerable variation in the length of college writing assignments. The primary goal in the Dartmouth College freshman composition program is to teach students to write a 1,000-word essay (about 4 pages). A professor from another selective college explains that his primary function is to help students face an 8-page (double spaced) essay without fear. The most common length for a college writing assignment is 5 pages, though you can expect the length of your college writing assignments to range from 1 to 20 pages.

Question #3: "I know some courses have over 300 students in them. Will professors really care or pay attention to what I write when they have so many students?"

The answer is *yes*, they do care. Your writing will be read carefully, and you must write with this in mind. Don't try to wing it! Even though you might attend large lecture courses, you will not be able to get away with general, unsubstantiated essays. Students at big universities agree. "Learn as much as you can about your topic. Professors and teaching assistants can detect immediately whether or not you know what you are writing about," recommends Vernyce, a history major at Ohio State. Kip echoes: "A few of my classmates felt they could weave together a string of 50-cent words and get an A. The words had a 10-cent effect. They got C's." Professors expect good diction in their students' writing. Many continue to ask for revisions until you have written exactly what you mean. An art history professor states, "I can only evaluate the specifics of what students write; I cannot speculate on their intent or what they might know or mean." Regardless of the size of the course, professors want logical and focused writing with a developed and substantiated argument.

Question #4: "How will I know what a professor really wants from a writing assignment?"

Learn how to evaluate composition assignments and how to analyze them by examining the language and asking the professor specific questions. Find the subject and verb in the description of the assignment; these will provide your focus. Does the assignment ask you to discuss, report, analyze, examine, compare, contrast, and/or justify? Determining this will help you adopt the appropriate voice and identify your audience.

"Listen for clues when professors first introduce writing assignments," suggests one student. "Sometimes professors will throw out ideas. In my history course, my professor mentioned that we could write and present a dramatic response to the assignment in place of the traditional essay. Since I'm a theater major, this hint saved my life."

Take time to discuss the assignment with a group of friends. Use them as a sounding board and ask them their thoughts on the topic. Never make the mistake of complaining to the professor that you don't understand what he or she wants. Ian, a college senior, laughs and comments, "Professors have one answer for that complaint: 'We want you to think; that's all.' "

Question #5: "What is the best way to approach an analytical essay?"

Develop a process that works for you. Sally, a college sophomore, talks about how she survived her first year of college writing by following guidelines set by her high school social studies teacher: "State what you want to prove as simply as you can; explain why your statement is true; keep questioning what you write and giving specifics to prove why your statements are true."

The first two points aid focus and clarity, while the third ensures logic and elaboration. Although the formula seems simplistic, it works. Sally's papers were praised repeatedly in her freshman year for clear, logical prose and for depth. She is quick to thank her high school social studies teacher for scribbling in the margins of her essays those once-dreaded words: *Why?* and *Proof.*

Question #6: "Will people help me with my writing in college?"

Marco, a UCLA junior, advises, "Pay attention to what professors tell you about your writing. Ask them to explain summary comments so that you can improve. Professors hate seeing the same writing mistakes over and over again." In seeking information about his weaknesses, Marco also received positive feedback about his writing strengths.

Most professors concur with this advice. "Whenever I have personal contact with a student," one sociology professor offers, "I am able to work more effectively evaluating his or her writing. So many students, in their eagerness for independence, allow themselves to get lost in the shuffle, only to find themselves not improving as writers."

Many courses have writing tutors trained to help you with your writing. Occasionally you will have to discuss your ideas and writing with your peer tutor before submitting a final paper. Tutors and others are on campus to help; take time to discover what writing support systems your college has: writing labs, writing centers, peer tutors, peer editors, writing tutors, writing associates.

Question #7: "Will I be able to talk to professors about my ideas and my writing?"

Chung, a sophomore from California, suggests, "Don't be intimidated by your professors." When papers are returned with numerous corrections, marginal comments, and a grade, it is difficult not to feel intimidated and inferior. Advanced students, however, urge freshmen and sophomores to take heart. "The process of specialization that evolves from the time you are a first-semester freshman to the time you are a senior or even a junior allows you to develop a common interest and commitment with professors," reports Brenda, a political science major. She adds, "Now that I have the base of knowledge and a more confident writing voice, I am relaxed sitting down with my professor and discussing my writing as one political scientist to another. I even find that the relationship we have on paper has changed. My professor's responses are more probing than critical. I find her asking me questions in the margins rather than making pointed critical statements. All of this has encouraged me to pursue our relationship." Another point to keep in mind: as you specialize, class size diminishes, fostering a more relaxed, personal professor-to-student rapport.

Question #8: "What one piece of writing advice would you give high school students?"

Ty, a freshman at Rochester Institute of Technology, responds unequivocally: "Write as much as you can in high school. Take as many courses as you can that demand good writing." Even though good college writing is different, the writing foundation and habits you develop in high school help you begin on the right foot. Myra, a University of Massachusetts sophomore, explains, "Professors were amazed that I could write a clear, logical four-page essay in the fall of my freshman year. I took extra English and social studies courses in high school because the teachers pushed writing. In college I had to learn to develop more complex thesis statements and provide more documentation, but at least I had the fundamentals."

"To become a comfortable and competent writer," advises Nalin, a college junior, "keep a journal! Nothing has helped me more to put thoughts on paper quickly and confidently." Even if you are not required to keep a journal, keep a record of reading and discussion reactions. It doesn't take any longer to write in a journal than it does to take conventional notes. Many students contend that journal writing is easier because it is less structured.

Let others help. Judson, a college junior, reveals his experience. "When I started exchanging papers with class-mates and then dormmates, I quickly learned that few people write correctly the first time. Even the people I thought were brilliant struggled with their writing. This was a big discovery for me." Exchanging your ideas and talking about them helps clarify your thoughts and lets you state them on paper simply.

Look for ways to write for fun. Vicky, a freshman from Virginia, offers this suggestion: "Our high school computer lab had an electronic bulletin board and I got hooked on it. By typing into the computer and transmitting the message to a bulletin board in another school, I became part of a writing network. I found people with common inter-ests, and the writing web grew. Several friends and I cre-ated our own network within our school. We would leave and receive messages during free periods." Bulletin board writing can be formal or informal, but to communicate, your writing must be clear and direct. Most important, bulletin boards are fun to use, and the only way to use them is by writing.

Question #9: "I write poems and short stories. Will I write only essays and reports in college? Will my creative writing skills help me?

Students feel strongly that creative writing prepares you for college writing. Suzanne, a creative writing major, insists, "I owe my good college writing to my journal and

---

Writing Schedule			
Due Date:			
Assignment:			
Writing Steps	Target Date	Completed	Notes/ Comments
Discuss Assignment	_____	_____	_____
Brainstorm Ideas	_____	_____	_____
Freewrite(s)	_____	_____	_____
Search for Focus	_____	_____	_____
Topic Sentence Outline	_____	_____	_____
Draft 1	_____	_____	_____
Revise Logic	_____	_____	_____
Peer Reading	_____	_____	_____
Draft 2	_____	_____	_____
Revise Elaboration	_____	_____	_____
Peer Reading	_____	_____	_____

fiction writing." Students concur: let creative writing help you become a better thinker and writer.

The writing voice and style developed through creative writing transfers to reports, business letters, and essay tests. "Don't forget that expository and analytical writing also require creative effort," observe several professors. In

Draft 3	_____	_____	_____
Revise Diction and Clarity	_____	_____	_____
Peer Reading	_____	_____	_____
Draft 4	_____	_____	_____
Revise Boldness and Audience	_____	_____	_____
Peer Reading	_____	_____	_____
Draft 5	_____	_____	_____
Final Revision	_____	_____	_____
Mechanics	_____	_____	_____
Peer Proofreading	_____	_____	_____
Final Draft	_____	_____	_____

Note: You will determine the order of your writing and revision steps and the exact timing of each draft. The important elements of this exercise, however, are planning, peer readings, and focused revisions. If you keep all of your writing assignments on grids, this should help you organize your time so that you don't become overwhelmed. See Chapter 2 for a detailed approach to the writing process and revision steps.

philosophy and sociology courses, you might be asked to solve moral dilemmas and social problems by role playing. A creative writing background helps you present your technical knowledge with creative insight. Zaneta, a German major, urges students to take a creative writing course early in their college years. "I learned to control language in a way that no other discipline had ever taught me. I know how to use language to create a specific mood."

Duane, a freshman at Ithaca College, describes creative writing as "writing without fear." Most creative writing courses encourage and even insist that students share their work. Students agree that sharing builds confidence: "The characters and conflicts were mine," continues Duane. "I was writing in my own style and not trying to imitate someone else's."

For Ethan, a junior at Colorado College, creative writing is "liberating. I am constantly experimenting with new styles and voices. Because of this, I'm more confident about writing in different settings; I'm able to communicate better when speaking. My creative writing has put me in touch with my emotions."

Creative writing also helps with reading. Doug, an American literature major, explains, "In creative writing, I spend a lot of time creating characters, setting, mood, and plot. When I'm reading for my literature courses, I'm more sensitive to these details and to the author's technique in revealing them. These skills have helped me in both class discussion and written analysis."

Question #10: "It takes me forever to write a paper. Will professors accept late assignments?"

Be careful. "If you are going to miss a deadline, talk to the professor," warns Clare, a sophomore from Florida. "Few offer an extension on the day an assignment is due. You have a chance, however, if you plan ahead and walk into the professor's office with a rough draft in hand."

You might also want to visit the writing center or lab. They may have strategies to help you speed up your writing process or work your way out of a particular writing jam.

One student explains how he counts backward from the due date and sets a rough schedule of deadlines. Professors and students recommend letting a paper sit for at least a day while you gain distance and objectivity about the assignment. To do this, you must be organized. A simple grid listing your writing and revision steps with target completion dates might keep you on target. See the sample on pages 144–45.

Conclusion

These 10 frequently asked questions mark a beginning. We hope they inspire you to keep asking questions of students when you get to college. These students have only recently made the transition from high school to college. Let their fresh experiences provide insight and comfort to you, as you begin to meet the challenges of college writing.

Professor

to

Student

Although advice on how to become a good writer abounds, actually becoming a good writer is not easy! You and other emerging writers have your own way of doing things, and in spite of the shared definition of good writing outlined in the previous chapters, there is not one route to becoming a good writer. In college, you will continue to define your writing process, but the challenge of fitting words to thoughts is lifelong.

Keep reminding yourself that there are no natural writers. In fact, the better the writer, the more time he or she commits to drafts and revision. By using and developing the writing habits and skills outlined in this book, you *can* become a good writer. Explains one professor, "Natural writing is a myth. No writers ever get it right the first time. Good writing comes hard." With time, patience, and commitment, you can reach your writing goals.

Having worked to become good writers themselves and having helped students with this task, professors have a lot to say about good writing. When asked, they most frequently make the following 10 recommendations to their students. This insider's information will help put you in the know, as you embark on your journey to become a college writer.

1. Develop a thesis. The thesis forms the essence of a well-conceived essay. In your essay and analytical writing, get to the point in the first paragraph. Without linking ideas to a focal statement, your essay will ramble. "Avoid the three-page introduction," urges a professor from a California university. If you are prone to long introductions, consider these two strategies: begin your introduction with a quotation that contains the heart of your argument; or, try to pose a research question that your essay will explore and answer.

Let's look at the first strategy. Beginning with a quotation forces you to address the ideas that will drive your essay. The actual words and/or images provided in the quotation will frame your thesis and topic sentences. You can also use words from the quotation to draw conclusions, ensuring cohesion and focus. For example, Verne uses Ralph Waldo Emerson's quotation to frame his four-page essay on youth and its role in reforming America: "So nigh is grandeur to our dust / So near to God is man / When Duty whispers low / Thou must / The youth replies, I can." Using Emerson's language, Verne develops the thesis, "We, the young, must prepare ourselves to answer that call of responsibility, to fulfill that promise 'I can.'" Verne's first topic sentence addresses a specific component of the quotation "You must first acquire the tool most vital to answering that call 'Thou Must': an education." In his conclusion, Verne returns to those key phrases when he writes, "I ask that you consider how our entire generation can best answer that call 'Thou Must.' How can we successfully fulfill that promise 'I Can'?"

By using the second strategy, posing a research question that your essay will explore and answer, your writing is immediately focused with key words and issues. For example, Rae begins her essay by asking her reader, "How has technology affected the Japanese work force?" Two terms—*technology* and *work force*—frame her essay; the word *how* establishes a cause/effect format. The word *Japanese* establishes a historical, cultural, and economic context. Rae's introduction poses a question that presents her focus for discussion.

Both the quotation and research question approaches offer key words to hold your essay together as well as to establish clear direction for elaboration.

2. Seek support. Seeking writing advice from peers and professors is not cheating. In fact, if you don't seek advice, you are doing yourself a disservice. Solicit responses from at least two different readers to determine if you have indeed communicated your ideas clearly and logically. With this input, you can return to your draft and tighten the order of sentences and paragraphs to construct an intelligent and thoughtful argument.

Don't be afraid to seek writing help. "Too many students wait until a crisis before they ask for help," suggests an American University professor. Keep in mind that most writers do not work in isolation; they confer all the time with friends and colleagues about their writing. Trained writing tutors and professionals can help you prevent disasters. Determine what services you might need and be sure they are available to you.

Seeking advice from peers enhances another essential skill: the ability to talk about one's writing. When you can identify and articulate weaknesses in your peers' writing, you become a better editor of your own writing. The development of this sixth sense carries good writing beyond the classroom. Pooling resources to produce "impassioned, detailed, and polished arguments" is an important lifelong good writing skill, suggests a professor from the University of Texas at Austin.

When getting help with your writing, ask specific questions, rather than making a general plea. Instead of saying, "I need help with this paper," you might want to try, "I need help with the topic sentences." Remember to maintain ownership of your paper; you want help with your writing, not someone to write the paper for you. Owning the final product means that you have to own the writing steps along the way.

3. Take risks. "When students tell me the writing topic I have assigned bores them, I turn it back to them as a challenge," explains one professor. When you feel passion or enthusiasm for a topic, you are far more likely to produce good writing. Try to find a way to get excited about your assignment. For example, if you are asked in an art history course to describe a building, you might want to do so from the perspective of a mouse rather than a person. Try to find a new angle to examine an old idea.

4. Be flexible. "Attitudes are more important than skills," reveals an English professor. Your willingness to encounter new ideas about writing is the universal expectation of college faculty. "Be flexible and willing to learn more about writing if you want to become a successful academic writer" explains Rebecca Howard, director of Colgate University's Interdisciplinary Writing Program. The first step to good writing is the willingness to accept criticism. This, however, means that you must separate your ego from your writing. If you can do this, you will view the opportunity to revise as a privilege and a complement to your ideas.

"Be willing to grow and change," writes Kathy Skubikowski, director of writing at Middlebury College. The skills you have now as a high school student, however solid they may be, won't suffice for the more sophisticated thinking you will be capable of in college. There, you are expected to have the patience and endurance to wrestle with words and ideas so that you can finally sit back knowing it is good writing and exclaim, 'That's it!' "

5. Treat writing as a game. Get hooked on writing, just as you might on a crossword puzzle; when you do, it becomes fun and not drudgery. See how many times you can change the verb in a sentence to one that is more dynamic. This adds energy to your writing. For example, take the sentence, "Fanny Lou Hamer was the real mother of the civil rights movement." Now, consider options that strengthen the verb: "Fanny Lou Hamer" "spirited . . . ," "Fanny Lou Hamer planted the seed . . . ," "Fanny Lou Hamer gave birth . . . ," "Fanny Lou Hamer mothered." These options create a richer image of the sharecropper. Try beginning a sentence in different ways, to give your writing variety. "As the real mother of the Civil Rights movement . . . ," "Unsung and unknown, Fanny Lou Hamer . . . ," "The civil rights movement finds its roots . . ." These options give you choices in your emphasis and style. The sentence you choose depends upon the thrust of your argument and your own style. See if there are different ways you can say the same word to avoid repetition. Take the word *movement* from the previous example, and list options to discover which word best fits your writing context: *crusade, campaign, struggle*. A dictionary or thesaurus can help you with this diction exercise.

6. Listen. Take in the advice and suggestions that peers and professors offer you. "Pay attention," advises Joseph Williams, director of writing at the University of Chicago. Also, pay attention to the Big Seven in developing good writing skills.

7. Read. "Read, read, read," urges Katherine Burnett of the Massachusetts Institute of Technology's writing program. Theresa Perri Ammirat, director of Connecticut College's writing center, adds, "Think about your reading. Become familiar with the many ways in which language can be used well." A reading regimen shows you what good writing is and provides a source of an active vocabulary. Read regularly and read anything from magazines to books, fiction to nonfiction, just as long as it's well written.

When you read, look for more than information; try to figure out the way an article, story, or an essay is written. When you discover pieces of writing that you like, save them so that you can bring models of good writing to college. They can help you organize your writing and develop a personal style. For example, many students have found that trying to imitate the clear, direct style of Ernest Hemingway has helped them with their writing. Imitating authors is not easy, but trying it can make you aware of different writing styles and give you a writing goal.

8. Write. Professors urge high school students to develop a writing regimen that includes both fiction and nonfiction. Seize every opportunity you can find to write. The writing need not be formal—keeping journals and writing lively letters demand your writing attention but are not as formal as essays or reports. One approach is to combine your reading and writing regimen; you might, for example, read a book and write a friend a good letter about it.

When a professor praises a piece of your writing, save it. Note the particular strengths of the piece and use it as a writing model for other courses, remembering that academic disciplines share common writing objectives. If you can stand it, save your writing disasters as well. They can make you more aware of your writing weaknesses.

9. Stay committed. When you say to yourself, "This is close enough, my professor will know what I mean," realize you have encountered a major pitfall that inhibits good writing. You cannot hover around an issue; you need to attack it and be precise. One professor explains that when he reads a general statement that isn't substantiated, he assumes one of two things: "Either this generality is the sum of the writer's knowledge, or the writer really does know more but hasn't written it." In either case, he asks for clarification and elaboration.

"The reader can never know what you meant to say. Your reader can only know what you have actually written," explains John McWilliams, an American literature professor. *The Student's Guide to Good Writing* stresses revision, and Professor McWilliam's comment reinforces the importance of writing clearly and logically. You cannot depend on your reader to sort out your ideas. This is your responsibility. The Big Seven, writing support services, word processing, and a writing schedule can all help you stay committed.

10. Be lively. "Try being a creative reporter, rather than a mechanical, duty-driven student," urges an economics professor. When reading 50 assignments on the same topic, professors appreciate something different. A bold alternative to the traditional essay can give you practice in creating a writing voice. Avoid boring your reader (and yourself!) with ideas that you think your professor wants to hear. Many professors recommend writing from your own experience and exploring unpopular or eccentric positions. Instead of writing a traditional report on the history of rock and roll, present the information from the point of view of an aged classical musician reflecting on this musical rebellion. There are endless creative approaches to an assignment. Take time to explore them.

Conclusion

Now you are ready. You know the specific expectations for good writing in college. You know how to make your writing better. You know the criteria of good writing. You have advice, recommendations, and answers that should help you slay your writing dragon.

Even though you are focusing on college writing, remember that you have a lifetime of writing ahead of you. Keep this in mind so that you don't expect too much of yourself during your first year of college. "This is your first year of production, not your last," reminds a professor.

Jean Sanborn of Colby College offers this parting advice: "Write. Experiment. Play with words. Think on paper. Share your writing with friends; talk about it. Revise (re-see). Rewrite. Evaluate your own writing." There are no quick fixes in this book or in the lifelong process of becoming a good writer. It's hard work, but it can be fun and there's plenty of help available. Now it's time to get started.

Recommended Texts

There are too many books about writing to name them all. However, from students, professors, and our own experience, we have compiled a list of favorite writing handbooks and texts that reflect the philosophy and recommendations of *The Student's Guide to Good Writing*.

You will find a section of writing books at most libraries and bookstores. Browsing through these texts will allow you to choose those that fit your needs. Keep an open mind as you explore them, and keep in mind that the list below is only intended to get you started. Don't be afraid to branch out on your own!

Biddle, Arthur. *Writer to Writer.* New York: McGraw-Hill, 1985.
Easy to read and understand, Biddle's book is useful for learning more about the writing process and practicing different writing formats. As the title suggests, Biddle talks to you as a writer. He offers ways for you to strengthen both your writing skills and your writing experience. From journal writing, to analysis, to research, to revision, Biddle's exercises are fresh and easy to work with on your own.

Corbett, Edward P. J. *The Little English Handbook: Choices and Conventions.* 5th ed. Glenview, Ill.: Scott, Foresman, 1987.

Our favorite because it is so comprehensive, *The Little English Handbook* provides information on manuscript format, grammar and punctuation, style, paragraphing, research papers, and more. The format and index of *The Little English Handbook* make it wonderfully accessible despite its broad scope. If you can only have one writing handbook or guide, this might be your best choice.

Elbow, Peter. *Writing without Teachers.* New York: Oxford University Press, 1979.

This book can help raise your awareness of your writing and your writing process. A less formal text than Biddle's *Writer to Writer, Writing without Teachers* offers a wonderful starting point for a group of writers to talk about their writing and themselves as writers. Elbow's book includes useful writing exercises for individuals or groups and explanations of how each exercise can improve your writing.

Elbow, Peter. *Writing with Power: Techniques for Mastering the Writing Process.* New York: Oxford University Press, 1981.

Elbow teaches you how to gain power over words and yourself as a writer. To this end, each chapter discusses a separate step of the writing process. Because Elbow doesn't want you to feel helpless or intimidated when you write, he offers specific strategies for overcoming writer's anxiety. Beyond these strategies, Elbow's recommendations for elaboration and revision are great.

Fulwiler, Toby. *College Writing.* Glenview, Ill: Scott, Foresman/Little Brown, 1988.

Fulwiler's book places writing in the context of the whole college experience. Drawing upon his students' journals, *College Writing* is personal and friendly. Fulwiler shares his own experiences as a writer and gives advice for writing assignments ranging from autobiographies to research papers. This text can help you further develop your writing formats and identify your own writing plan.

Gibaldi, Joseph, and Walter S. Achtert. *MLA Handbook for Writers of Research Papers*. 3d ed. New York: Modern Language Association of America, 1988.
The *MLA Handbook* has more information than Strunk and White's *Elements of Style*. Offering a succinct explanation of footnote and bibliography entries, this source is the official style sheet for many colleges and universities. Its overview of grammar rules comes with examples to help clarify questions about usage and application.

Krevisky, Joseph, and Jordan L. Linfield. *The Bad Speller's Dictionary*. New York: Random House, 1967.
If you do not plan to word process and use a spell check, you might want to buy this dictionary. Although there are similar texts on the stands, *The Bad Speller's Dictionary* helpfully lists words in the left-hand column that are often misspelled and matches them with the correct spelling on the right. This allows you to easily approach a word that you are unsure how to spell.

Meyer, Herbert E., and Jill M. Meyer. *How to Write*. Washington, D.C.: Storm King Press, 1986.
The Meyers' book is full of ideas and examples about how to develop a writing process. Clear, direct, and friendly, the book presents writing in four parts: "Organizing for the Job," "Turning out a First Draft," "Polishing the Product," and "Ready, Set, Go."

Strunk, William, and E. B. White. *The Elements of Style*. 3d ed. New York: Macmillan, 1979.
Tried and tested, this is the writing handbook that your parents probably used. And it's still useful! Strunk and

161

White's book answers questions on specific writing problems: when to use "affect" versus "effect," where to place commas, and how to select the correct pronoun. This handbook is a useful resource when you revise for diction, clarity, and mechanics.

Venolia, Jan. *Write Right: A Desktop Digest of Punctuation, Grammar, and Style*. Rev. ed. Berkeley, Calif.: Ten Speed Press/Periwinkle Press, 1988.

More animated and easier to read than *Elements of Style*, this handbook may be used for advice on punctuation, mechanics, grammar, style, and confused and abused words. When revising for diction, clarity, and mechanics, a resource like *Write Right* is invaluable.

Zinsser, William. *On Writing Well: An Informal Guide to Writing Non-fiction*. 3d ed., rev. and enl. New York: Harper & Row, 1985.

An excellent resource, Zinsser's book discusses the seven elements of good writing in depth. Because Zinsser's approach is not overbearing, you can learn a good deal about the components of good writing quickly and easily. Zinsser uses helpful examples to illustrate how to approach everything from sports writing to criticism.

The Right Word II. 2d ed., rev. Boston: Houghton Mifflin, 1983.

The Right Word is a concise thesaurus that helps you find the best words to communicate your ideas. What makes this thesaurus special is that rather than listing all possible synonyms, it presents word choices that address the most important meanings of the original word. When revising for clarity and diction, a resource such as this is invaluable.

Index

Index

Other Books of Interest from the College Board

003349 *Coping with Stress in College,* by Mark Rowh. The first book to examine the stresses specifically related to college life, this provides students with practical advice and guidelines for coping with stress. ISBN: 0-87447-334-9, $9.95

003357 *Countdown to College: Every Student's Guide to Getting the Most Out of High School,* by Zola Dincin Schneider and Phyllis B. Kalb. A one-of-a-kind book to help every teenager do well in high school and be prepared for college. ISBN: 0-87447-335-7, $9.95.

003055 *How to Help Your Teenager Find the Right Career,* by Charles J. Shields. Step-by-step advice and innovative ideas to help parents motivate their children to explore careers and find alternatives suited to their interests and abilities. ISBN: 0-87447-305-5, $12.95

002482 *How to Pay for Your Children's College Education,* by Gerald Krefetz. Practical advice to help parents of high school students, as well as of young children, finance their children's college education. ISBN: 0-87447-248-2, $12.95

003373 *Index of Majors, 1989-90.* Lists over 500 majors at the 3,000 colleges and graduate institutions, state by state, that offer them. ISBN: 0-87447-337-3, $14.95 (Updated annually)

002911 *Profiles in Achievement,* by Charles M. Holloway. Traces the careers of eight outstanding men and women who used education as the key to later success. (Hardcover, ISBN: 0-87447-291-1, $15.95); 002857 paperback (ISBN: 0-87447-285-7, $9.95)

002598 *Succeed with Math,* by Sheila Tobias. A *practical* guide that helps students overcome math anxiety and gives them the tools for mastering the subject in high school and college courses as well as the world of work. ISBN: 0-87447-259-8, $12.95

003225 *Summer on Campus,* by Shirley Levin. A comprehensive guide to more than 250 summer programs at over 150 universities. ISBN: 0-87447-322-5, $9.95

003039 *10 SATs: Third Edition.* Ten actual, recently administered SATs plus the full text of *Taking the SAT,* the College Board's official advice. ISBN: 0-87447-303-9, $9.95

002571 *Writing Your College Application Essay,* by Sarah Myers McGinty. An informative and reassuring book that helps students write distinctive application essays and explains what colleges are looking for in these essays. ISBN: 0-87447-257-1, $9.95

002474 *Your College Application,* by Scott Gelband, Catherine Kubale, and Eric Schorr. A step-by-step guide to help students do their best on college applications. ISBN: 0-87447-247-4, $9.95

To order by direct mail any books not available in your local bookstore, please specify the item number and send your request with a check made payable to the College Board for the full amount to: College Board Publications, Department M53, Box 886, New York, New York 10101-0886. Allow 30 days for delivery. An institutional purchase order is required in order to be billed, and postage will be charged on all billed orders. Telephone orders are not accepted, but information regarding any of the above titles is available by calling Publications Customer Service at (212) 713-8165.